UNCHAINED!

by
Mac Gober

KENNETH

COPELAND

PUBLICATIONS

The accounts depicted in this book are factual and based upon the true life story of Mac Gober. Names have been purposely altered to protect the anonymity of certain persons and safeguard the sensitive nature of isolated events. The dialogue is based upon fact. The bylaws of the Tribe of Judah motorcycle ministry, of which Gober is president for the state of Alabama, specifically declare, "No individual in this ministry will violate the confidence of any persons or organization to incriminate, convict, or aid in any area of law enforcement. We are committed to staying neutral in these situations." We have taken this pledge to avoid offending and alienating the members of the motorcycle clubs of America whom we are seeking to reach with the love of Jesus Christ.

Unless otherwise noted, all scripture is from the *King James Version* of the Bible.

Unchained!

ISBN-10 1-57562-041-3   30-0810
ISBN-13 978-1-57562-041-1

17 16 15 14 13 12   14 13 12 11 10 9

© 1998 by Mac Gober
P.O. Box 310
Autaugaville, AL 36003

Kenneth Copeland Publications
Fort Worth, TX 76192-0001

For more information about Kenneth Copeland Ministries, visit kcm.org or call 1-800-600-7395 (U.S. only) or +1-817-852-6000.

To . . .

Jesus, Savior and Lord of my life.

My beautiful and wonderful wife, who is my best friend (next to Jesus, of course).

Three of the greatest kids on this planet — Rachel, Caleb, and Joshua. I adore you and am having a great time growing up with you.

All the broken lives that Jesus has healed through the Canaan Land Boys' Home.

Contents

Foreword

I've known Mac Gober for a number of years. In 1992, after Mac shared the testimony you are about to read, I witnessed the largest response to any invitation to the lost ever given in one of our Believers' Conventions. I believe that was one of the strongest soul-winning anointings I have ever seen in my life. Mac's testimony is honest. It's powerful. And it's compelling.

This is not just a story of how the gospel plucked a life from certain destruction. It's much more than that. It's the story of how God's Word totally transformed a life and produced a man with a mission. I can't remember anything that has made me laugh harder than the stories of Mac's early days as a baby Christian. He didn't know anything about the Bible. He knew churches had different names, but didn't know they were split over the Bible. And he was so full of the love of Jesus, he tripped over religious traditions in his urgency to tell about a precious and powerful relationship with a living God.

A more joyous story of victory would be hard to find. But to get to that joy, you have to walk with Mac through some of the pain of his brokenness. Even in telling of the confusion and eventual brutality of his rebellion, Mac leaves no room for darkness to get glory.

Jesus came to heal the brokenhearted. And Mac was a prime candidate. Mac's home was ravaged by alcohol, abuse and divorce. Without the gospel, there was nothing to fill the growing emptiness. Hoping to find some direction and purpose, he fought for his country in Vietnam, only to watch his buddies die and his nation reject her heroes. Back home, the sense of rejection and his seething anger pulled him into the brotherhood of outlaw bikers.

Here we have a window into a world which many of us have never seen, but which has affected each of us in some way. We see a young man abandoned by his dad, trying to grow up by fighting in a conflict that would recognize no heroes. We get a glimpse inside the world of the outlaw biker, and how it offered a form of acceptance and a substitute hope for the dashed dreams of a life that seemed beyond God's forgiveness and love.

There may be times you will wonder if you are reading about someone who is beyond God's reach. Mac's conscience was numbed. Drugs had made a scrambled mess of his brain. He was cool and cruel in his brutality. You may ask if the gospel could really be, for someone like Mac Gober, the power of God unto salvation for every one who believes.

But as you grow to understand Mac and the amazing depth of God's love for him and through him, you'll understand more of God's mercy and grace for you and me. *Unchained!* will give you an inside view of one of those whom Jesus said are invited to the wedding feast while they were still in the highways and hedges. Mac is a last days' warrior, once trained by Satan to advance the kingdom of darkness, but now crashing the gates of hell with the awesome power of the love of God. He often refers to the promise of John 1:12, "But as many as received him, to them gave he power to become the sons of God, even to them that believe on his name." He has told me the day he was saved was like an atom bomb full of love and grace exploding inside a lost and undone young man on the dark side of San Diego. The power of God was activated in him, his desires changed immediately and he became a new person from the inside out.

Today Mac Gober is one of the most powerful men of God anywhere in this world. I have ridden motorcycles with Mac. I have ministered with him and witnessed with him. I've called on him when I needed help. Mac has always been there. He's been there for the men and women and young people at Canaan Land and at the Fort Courage summer camps. I've seen the fruit of Mac's 20 years as a believer.

Years ago Mac's friends were locking him in barns to protect him and the world from his insanely violent outbursts. Now, through Canaan Land Ministries, he and his wife, Sandra, provide havens of recovery and discipleship to men and women off the streets. The old Mac left behind trails of bruised bodies and broken lives. Now wherever Mac goes — prisons, outlaw biker clubs, churches or conventions — he leaves growing thousands of reborn lives and ministers of the gospel in his wake. As a young man, what little Mac heard about God was quickly lost in the confusion and pain of his home life. Now, each summer at his Fort Courage youth camp, Mac gives young men and women the courage and motivation to hang with God and His

Word through all the troubles and challenges life can throw at them.

Yes, the "gospel of Christ [the Anointed One]...is the power of God unto salvation to every one that believeth; to the Jew first, and also to the Greek," as Romans 1:16 says. Any one who has access to the gospel has access to the power of God. When the human spirit grabs hold of the Word of God, that Word begins to grow. The power of God comes out of the gospel and starts working right there on the inside of that person. And as long as he or she doesn't turn it off, it will make something good grow.

The power of the gospel was wonderfully illustrated in a story Mac told me about his first few days as a new believer. He had gone back to his old neighborhood to share with the guys what had happened to him. There in the middle of the night, a man started screaming in the street like a maniac, threatening to kill everybody in the neighborhood. That neighborhood was not the place to do that. Many mornings the first rays of sunlight fell on someone who had been murdered the night before. A couple of the guys Mac was with started loading crossbows to go do the man in.

Even though he was less than two weeks old as a believer, the power of God that was exploding inside of Mac couldn't let that happen. He walked out into the night, and placing his hulking body between the man and the loaded crossbows, Mac told him, "Apparently you're going through a bad time. You need to just go on back in, because let me tell you something, God loves you."

Behind him, the guys were hollering, "Get out of the way we are going to shoot him." But filled with the love and power of God, Mac said, "No, you'll have to shoot me. Nobody's going to die anymore." He knew very little about the Bible, but Mac began to pray with that man the best he knew how to pray. The presence of God shooting through Mac hit the man who moments earlier couldn't think straight and was acting like a maniac. He began to cry, shut up, turned around and walked back into the house.

That's the power of this gospel we live and minister. This book is your appointment to be refreshed and renewed in the full power of God's promises to you and those you love. Read it with your heart open wide. Let it stir your faith to believe for someone you love that needs God. God's Word planted deeply into the human spirit will change anyone. All they have to do is receive it. No burden or yoke of bondage can stand against it. Just like it did for Mac Gober, this gospel is the promise of God to anyone who needs to be *Unchained!*

Kenneth Copeland

Mac Gober As Seen by a Friend and Admirer

Mac Gober and I met sometime around 1985, and I remember one experience early in our friendship that made a tremendous impact on me.

It was a warm, sunny afternoon in Montgomery, Alabama. Mac gave me a call and invited me to come with him to a young men's correctional facility outside the city, where he had been asked to speak. I came from work in a three-piece suit; Mac had on jeans. He didn't tell me what kind of chapel service this was going to be, and I was looking forward to hearing what he had to say to these young men who had taken the wrong road so early in their lives.

What I didn't know was that the week before this same crowd had heckled a local pastor out of the chapel and wouldn't let him speak. In fact, they had a reputation for running speakers out on a regular basis.

So when we walked into the chapel they thought this was going to be an encore, and a few of them began yelling out comments.

But Mac wasn't intimidated. This giant of a man, robust like a bull but with all the gentleness that comes with a heart broken by God — he knew exactly where these guys were coming from and what motivated them. He had been there, too.

And so he told them his story — a traumatic childhood, Vietnam, the motorcycle gangs, dealing drugs. Within five minutes these men were so riveted on what he was saying that you could have heard a pin drop in the stillness. He was speaking right to them — to their pain, their anger, their disappointment — all the wasted years. He had earned the right to be heard.

In the next thirty-five minutes he went on to tell them how Jesus Christ had rescued him, taken his pain, and set him free. Jesus could set them free, too.

Then Mac invited them to come forward in what I consider the toughest altar call I've ever heard. He concluded it by saying, "I don't want any temporary 'jailhouse conversions' here. I only want you to come to the front of this room if you really want to change the direction of your life forever."

I remember thinking, "He's making it so hard — I wonder if anyone will come."

In that next moment the altar was overflowing with young men going forward to find a new beginning. I was amazed to see some of the biggest, roughest looking guys breaking down in tears as the Lord touched their hearts. Men of all races and backgrounds crowded together, kneeling and praying. That day the Lord used the broken pieces of Mac's life to bring salvation, the baptism of the Holy Spirit, and a fresh start to so many.

Since then I've gone into full-time ministry at the Christian Broadcasting Network and moved to Virginia Beach. I've had the opportunity to see many great men of God who have appeared on our broadcasts or spoken at conferences. But over the years I've known Mac, I'd have to say he is among the three most dedicated Christian leaders I know today. I have the utmost respect and admiration for him and his ministry, and I consider it a privilege to count him as a good friend.

Because of Mac's love and understanding of people who are hard to love, I've invited him to be a featured speaker each year at CBN's Vietnam Veterans Conferences — one of our most powerful annual ministry events. His testimony is so strong even the most hardened vets are touched by his love and compassion as he shares what the Lord has done for him since Vietnam.

The story you are about to read in this book will give you hope. No matter how terrible your life has been — you're never beyond God's reach. Wherever you are He can bring you back, heal your wounds, and make your life into something wonderful. And He can use you to touch others.

Rob Hartley, Vice President of Development
The Christian Broadcasting Network

Background

In 1947, the year of my birth, the American Motorcycle Association (the AMA) was having a membership party in Riverside, California. A pack of independent bikers crashed the party and caused a riot. A Riverside sheriff inflamed the situation by blaming a bunch of "crazy kids" for the disturbance. Newspapers and media reports labeled the rebel bikers as "outlaws" and made a clear distinction, in their words, between them and the wholesome motorcycle clubs comprised of decent, law-abiding citizens. The conservative AMA had characterized 99 percent of all motorcycle enthusiasts as clean-living folks, enjoying the love and laughter of motorcycle fun and freedom. According to them, the remaining 1 percent of motorcyclists were renegade hoodlums who roamed the highways and byways of America stirring up trouble and raising hell. The slanderous publicity birthed the label of the "One Percenters" and helped drive a wedge between their outlaw clubs and the rest of society — so was born the mystique and notorious reputation of the outlaw bikers. The distinction and negative press created an atmosphere of contempt and alienation that only helped to contribute to the renegade mentality of the outlaw biker clubs who prided themselves on being outside the mainstream of society and bent on doing everything and anything they wanted outside the bounds of the law.

Acknowledgments

Pat Robertson has helped and supported the Caanan Land Ministries for years. Oral Roberts taught me that God is my source, to plant seeds away from myself, and to expect miracles. Dr. Jerry Savelle believed in me and supported me; he continues to promote Caanan Land by serving on its honorary board. Kenneth Copeland is a special friend, given to me by God at a time when I needed his friendship most. Dick Lovelady's unselfish love for me as a young minister is the reason I am here today; I will always be thankful to him. Evelyn Alexander is my spiritual mom who loves me unconditionally. Jackie Mitchum Yockey is one of God's special agents who works without seeking the limelight. Ben Priest and I have a special patch sewn in the collar of our colors, and it will keep us close for the rest of our lives (TOJFFTOJPB). Rob and Judy Hartley are two of the strongest, purest people I know. Pastors Steve and Denice Vickers of Christian Life Church in Montgomery, Alabama, have ministered to me and my family for ten years. Mike Murdock, whom I owe so much for his constant love and support who taught me to keep my eyes on the grapes and not on the giants. Keith Johnson, who was a role model of what a minister should be not only behind the pulpit, but also with his family. Daddy Larry and Mamma Joy Blassingame, thanks for all

your years of unselfish love for helping me raise
Rachel, Caleb and Joshua. Dee Melendez worked so
hard on the manuscript of my book. I could not have
done it without her. My board members are the most
loyal, supportive folks in the world. Finally, the staff of
Canaan Land is the best bunch of people any man of
God could want.

Preface

The squad filed out into the darkness around midnight with Sergeant Jacobs walking point. Roger was in the eleventh position, behind Paterson, but he didn't like it one bit — not because Jacobs was taking his position that night, but because Jacobs was a little too sure of himself for his own good.

The squad moved quickly through the night. The black vault was sprinkled with thousands of shining stars. In a few minutes, the men reached the wide dike leading out to the fishing village they were to patrol that night.

Malevolent swarms of hungry bugs batted about their heads, oblivious to the thick coating of oily repellent smeared on their faces and necks. Jacobs led the squad in a brisk pace down the path past several intersecting dikes and occasional stands of trees. The only noise was the gentle swishing sound of men moving along the dike.

Accustomed to walking point, Roger didn't like the unfamiliar feeling of being so far back in the pack. He was keyed up and edgy as he kept pace with the column of men. "They're going too fast," he thought. "Jacobs is pushing the squad too fast...He's in too much of a hurry." The briskness of Jacob's pace agitated Roger. The squad was a couple hundred meters from the outskirts of the village. Roger had a vague, ominous feeling. "He's got to slow this race down and take his time." He wanted to say something, but hesitated. His concerns were nagging him. Then he sensed it. Some inner instinct triggered a premonition of impending danger. His body was suddenly electrified by a strange prickly sensation crawling up his spine. "I've got to warn them!" The thought shot through his mind as the squad stepped into the killing zone of an L-shaped ambush.

I sat riveted to my seat at that first Christian Broadcasting Network Vietnam Veterans' Conference as Bill Kimball recounted the haunting testimony of Roger Helle, a decorated Marine who had suffered through the brutal ordeal of seeing his entire squad wiped out in Vietnam. I had heard countless sermons and moving messages over the years, but few had gripped me as the words I was hearing at that moment. I had been invited to speak at that CBN conference by Rob Hartley, one of the leaders of CBN. A few months before, Roger Helle and Rob had discussed the need for a healing conference to address the lingering wounds of the Vietnam veteran community. I had been invited to that conference as a main speaker opening night to minister to those who were still hurting, but as I sat there that night with my attention in a vise grip, I realized that the words I was hearing were ministering in a special way to me.

The story of Roger's squad was set twenty years before and half a world away, but the message was speaking to me at that moment right from the heart of God. Without knowing it, I had stepped into an ambush which God had prepared just for me.

KaBLAAMM!

A violent flashbulb explosion erupted behind the squad hurling the last three men into the paddy water like rag dolls. Roger's entire life flashed through his mind in instant replay. Splash! He landed on his back in the paddy water. His ears were ringing, but otherwise he was unhurt.

The curtain of blackness was rent by flashes. Marines screamed from hits.

Rifles crackled and stuttered in a chaotic cacophony which grew in intensity until it reached a maniacal clap.

Zzzzzzssst Thuo!... KRUNCH! A B-40 rocket opened up the dike a few meters away, pelting the surrounding paddy water with thousands of geysers from falling mud.

Men screamed as rounds thudded into their bodies.

"Where's my rifle?" Roger freaked as he groped along the paddy's muddy bottom with his hands. He couldn't find it. He half-crawled, half-swam through the muck to the edge of the dike and dug his hands into the mud to secure himself.

Green and red tracers scratched fluorescent lines across the field in a perverse Morse code. A captured M-60 raked the dike with angry bursts. Bullets spit into the bank, kicking up clods of dirt that fell around him. Roger was submerged in the paddy with his head just above water, half-buried among the rice shoots.

The hailstorm of fire sputtered off, then stopped.

He could hear the gurgling sound of a Marine gasping for air. "Help me...Please, help me," the faint whimper floated in the air. Roger was terrified and trembling. He was wet and shivering from cold.

Another guy a few feet from him was moaning softly: "It hurts."

"Ssssh," Roger whispered.

"Oh, God, it hurts bad."

Roger canted his head slightly, straining to listen. He could hear the muffled sounds of men approaching. They were speaking in clipped Vietnamese phrases. He pulled himself along the side of the dike through the stagnant water and cupped the wounded Marine's mouth with his hand. There were two of them lying next to each other. They had been behind him when the command-detonated mine went off, blowing them off the dike also. Both were bleeding profusely from multiple shrapnel wounds. Their eardrums were ruptured and leaking blood from the concussion.

The sounds were getting closer. "Nice work, Van," he heard one of them say. "Check the bodies...Gather anything we can use," another instructed.

"Oh, God, I don't want them to find me!" Roger shuddered as an avalanche of panic overwhelmed him. He quickly covered the heads of the two wounded Marines with some rice shoots, then pushed himself back from the bank as far as he could reach and still hold on. Through the rice shoots he could just make out the ghoulish silhouettes of VC scavengers moving along the dike, stopping to kick a body or stooping to gather weapons.

"This one's still alive, Sergeant Tran. What do we do with the wounded?" one of the soldiers asked.

"You know what to do with them, fool!" another snapped.

"Auughh." Roger heard the anguished rush of air from a wounded Marine as one of the VC finished him off.

"We must hurry...before the helicopters come!" one of them ordered. "Quickly, comrades!"

The VC were talking and laughing softly as they hurriedly went about the grisly business of stripping the dead bodies of personal effects — watches, wedding rings, wallets.

"Nice watch, Trung," Roger heard one of them say.

"Stick..." Roger thought he heard the plaintive voice of Scroggins, pleading in the darkness.

There was a pistol shot and then another as the VC systematically stilled the remaining twitching bodies.

"Filthy Marine dogs!" one of them scowled.

Agonizing moments passed in terror-filled suspense — then the ghostly apparitions moved off into the night. A worried silence followed in the wake of their departure. The night was tomb quiet as Roger waited and listened, afraid to move. "God, it burns so much!" one of the wounded muttered.

"It'll be okay. Just hang in there," Roger urged.

"I'm so tired," the other spoke.

"Stay awake! Don't fall asleep! Listen to me! You've got to try to stay awake!" Roger pleaded with him. Both were losing blood fast and slipping into shock. He couldn't lie there clinging to the dike forever or they would die. He had to chance it. He took a deep breath and mustered enough resolve to pull himself up out of the slop to check out the squad.

Ten men were sprawled along the dike with their limbs splayed in grotesque angles. He checked each one for signs of life, but they were all dead — riddled by bullets and shrapnel wounds. Several had their throats slit. He found Sergeant Jacobs half-naked with his boots off and his fatigue shirt removed. His chalk-white chest was smeared with blood from some of the twenty-seven rounds that hit him.

Miraculously, Roger found the radio still intact. It was under the body of Paterson, who was slumped over it backward on the slope of the dike with his head partially submerged under paddy water. Roger turned him over and pulled his body up onto the dike. He then removed the radio pack, adjusted the squelch knob and keyed the hand mike. His hand was shaking badly and his voice quivering, but somehow he managed to call in.

Roger was reeling from aftershock and emotional exhaustion as he headed back in the truck. "Jacobs shouldn't have been pulling point," he thought to himself as he sat hunched over in the seat. "The squad was my responsibility! If only I had warned them."

He spent a fitful night rehearsing the lightning events that had wiped out his squad in the blink of an eye.

The following morning he returned to his base camp — back to the painful reminders of his friends lying where he had left them. He had come back, but they hadn't and that knowledge haunted him.

In the loneliness of their compound Roger's emotions caved in around him, burying him under an oppressive burden of guilt. It clawed at his mind, gnawed at his heart, set heavy in his throat, like something pushing down hard on his chest — guilt because he had made it and they hadn't, guilt that he hadn't reacted faster, guilt that he hadn't said something, guilt because he was relieved to be alive even though his buddies were dead. It was a heaviness from which he couldn't escape. It dogged his every move, filling every space of his life like an evil presence. He couldn't shake the anguish of knowing that he was alive and his friends weren't coming back, and he would carry that burden of guilt for years.

Bill had been ministering on "Overcoming Survivor's Guilt." He was talking about the invisible duffel bag of guilt that many of us quietly carried home from Vietnam years before — guilt dumped on us by an ungrateful nation who sent her sons to war and held them in contempt when they returned; guilt for things some of us did in moments of confusion or blind rage; guilt for leaving our friends behind; guilt for making it back home when so many more noble than we lost their lives in the rice paddies and jungles of Vietnam.

The anguish in Roger's testimony mirrored my own troubled soul and the guilt and pain I had secretly carried for years. The words I heard triggered pent-up memories and emotions that I had long buried. I had come to the CBN conference as a minister with every intention of ministering to others. I had also come as a "well-adjusted Christian" who had already experienced the power of Jesus Christ to change lives. But I found myself sitting there dazed, asking myself over and over, "Why are you feeling this way? What's goin' on, Mac?

You've already been saved. You've already put this behind you — haven't you?" I knew in my heart, though, that I really hadn't, and I knew that God was speaking to me, and I couldn't hold back the tears any longer. As I sat there that day with hot tears streaming down my face and a tide of long-suppressed memories flooding my mind, I was brought face to face with the reality of just what the Lord had done for me. I sat there stunned by the revelation of how much hurt and hate He had delivered me from. He led me to that conference that day to touch my own wounded heart. As I turned to glance around that room my eyes met the weeping faces of my brothers-in-arms, middle-aged now and some still broken in body, and our hearts were overwhelmed with the love of God. I sat there in the midst of a company of men and women who had weathered so much suffering in their lives, with a profound sense of thankfulness for what Jesus had done for us.

I think that it was at that pivot point in my life that the seeds for this book were sown. A host of friends, like Rob Hartley, had encouraged me over the years to put my testimony into a book, but the tumblers had never seemed to line up in my mind until the CBN conference.

A wise old man of God had counseled me years earlier, "Don't write the book just yet, Mac. Be patient. You need to let several years pass after your salvation. Then you can write your book when the whole story can be told." I know in my heart that the events that came together that day at the CBN Vietnam Veterans Conference were the finishing touches that needed to happen before this story could really be told.

C H A P T E R 1

The Sins of the Fathers

• • •

The driving torrent of rain suddenly lifted. The ensuing silence was almost deafening. It had been pouring steadily for six days. Except for the occasional patter of droplets trickling down through the thick vegetation, the night had grown quiet — too quiet. I squinted my eyes and carefully wiped the moisture from my face. My eyes darted back and forth in an attempt to catch any hint of suspicious movement along the river, avoiding the mistake of staring at one spot too long. It was 0430 — one of those pre-dawn hours when the night blackness often played tricks with the eyes, when objects and shadows could easily create figments in the mind and toy with fertile imaginations.

That's when I spotted it. "There's something moving out there," I told myself. Then it was gone. "No, there it is again." I was sure of it this time. Drifting lazily midstream was a tangle of clotted brush and branches.

I took careful aim at the knotted bundle of vegetation floating by. Odds were that it was only one of the many pieces of jungle debris flushed from the dense mountains upstream, but I couldn't take any chances. It could be mined. Two hundred meters more and it would hit the pontoon bridge downstream I was helping protect from sabotage.

I sighted in with my M-14 and slowly squeezed off a shot.

KAWHOOM! The river was suddenly illuminated by a bright orange flash sending a towering plume into the air and showering my position with a blanket of mud and water.

The blackness had only been thrown back for a moment, then the darkness returned. The rains returned as well. Somewhere across the river a lone flare hissed overhead, bathing the river in an eerie green glow. Tendrils of burnt cordite crept toward me through the rain. *Ta tow tow tow.* In the distance, the reassuring stutter of an M-60 punctuated the rhythmic cadence of the falling rain. I hunkered down in my position and tried to shake off the damp chill as a hard rain began to fall. I was alone again in my jungle cocoon — alone with my thoughts and fears.

The rainy season was miserable. The torrential deluge of the monsoon rains was one of the worst experiences for any grunt. I sat shivering in my sodden firing position, chilled to the bone in soaked fatigues that clung to my body like wet sheets. I was a portrait of misery in the slop of that fighting hole as a steady shower filtered through the thick covering of jungle foliage.

There were long stretches in Nam when the heat and humidity were unbearable, when you felt like you were being slowly basted on a grill. That was during the dry, hot season. There were basically two seasons in Vietnam — one wet, one dry. We cursed both of them. If you weren't enduring the purgatorial agony of the hot season, you were weathering the misery of the monsoon rains.

It had been the sixth consecutive day of rain as I crouched down by the bank of the Da Nang River waiting for Charlie to make one of his nocturnal appearances. Sitting there shivering in my soaked fatigues, I felt like I had been dropped into a world better suited for amphibians or creatures with gills than for human beings.

The hot season had passed several weeks before, bringing a return of the rains. The rains were inter-mittent at first, almost tentative, then they hit with a vengeance. In short order, my area of operation had been transformed into a muddy mess. Almost daily towering, blue-black thunderheads massed over the mountains of Laos before they began their relentless march to the sea — pregnant cloudbursts that released torrential sheets of rain that hit the flesh with biting stings. At times the mountains around Da Nang were veiled with toneless gray mists of drizzle and fog. At other times they were assaulted with thunderous claps of lightning and torrential rain that sent millions of incoming droplets that hit the ground like miniature bomb bursts, churning the red dirt into a muddy soup. Nothing escaped the near constant drumming — sandbags, bunkers, poncho liners, canvas, men. Relentless lines pelted cans strung along the perimeter wire and corrugated roofing of our compound, sounding like a thousand snare drums. Every depression, every rut, soon pooled with water. Eventually everything started to rot and mildew from the constant damp — even men's nerves.

On those long, solitary night ambushes I had lots of time to think and reflect. Only a few weeks earlier during the dry season, I had sat in that same hole cursing the local coalition of hungry mosquitoes hovering about my head in search of exposed patches of flesh upon which to feed. Sometimes it seemed that the Da Nang River was the birthing place for the mother of all mosquitoes. I'd sat there in the oppressive humidity with rivulets of sweat coursing down my neck, afraid to move or slap for fear of alerting any VC who might be moving downriver through the blackness.

At that moment of personal misery I would have gladly traded a dry night for the one I was drowning in. I didn't know how much more of the perpetual drenching I could take. I spent countless hours fantasizing of going home. How ironic, I thought, that I had enlisted in the first place, to escape the pressure of a troubled life back home.

Only a few years before, I practically begged my mother to sign the enlistment papers from the recruitment office giving me permission to enlist underage. I was sixteen then and barely nineteen now. I'd only been in the "armpit," what we sarcastically called Nam, for three months, but it seemed that I had been fighting my own personal war for a long time.

I was born in Jasper, Alabama, in 1947. I wasn't born into a picture-perfect family. My life was a fractured version of the American dream. My family wasn't cut out of the mold of "Ozzie and Harriet" or "Father Knows Best," but was what you could best describe as your not so typically dysfunctional family. I suppose you could say that I did "hard time" as a kid.

I spent my growing years steeped in strife and nurtured on neglect.

My dad was a strong, muscular man — a steel worker who was as tough as re-bar. He worked hard and drank harder. Because of him, we never knew what stability meant. Due to the demands of his job, we lived a tumbleweed existence — shuffling like nomads from one town to the next. We never settled down. We never experienced a sense of belonging before the job would end, our family would be uprooted once again, and we would head down the road to the next job. It was nothing for me to change schools two or three times a year.

My dad had carried home a sea bag full of problems from World War II. He had served aboard the USS *Lexington*, fighting the Japs in the South Pacific. He was aboard the carrier when it took several direct hits and was in danger of sinking. The klaxon sounded the call to abandon ship, but the explosions had gutted the interior of the carrier. My dad found himself trapped below decks in the ruptured bowels of the ship amid twisted beams and buckled decking. A bunch of terrified Marines were clawing their way through the tangle in an attempt to find their way to the upper decks when they found my dad pinned under some wreckage. My dad shouted to them, "You guys get me out of here and I'll show you the way out!" They pried the steel off of him and he showed them the way through the maze of passageways until they were able to jump overboard. He spent quite a while in the sea until they were picked up. Amazingly, the rescue ship was hit a few days later and he was thrown overboard once again.

The claustrophobic nightmare of being trapped below decks, amid the screams of men drowning behind watertight doors, of the deafening explosions of armor-piercing bombs, of smoke-filled passageways, of burning flesh, of steel decking so hot it glowed red, and of treading water in shark-infested seas all took a heavy toll on my dad.

My dad was what you could call "a driven man." His anger was rooted in his own repressed past — a past that had been gaining on him for a long while. The stress that had been seething inside him for years began to surface in unpredictable flashes of anger. It was the same strain of delayed stress that I was destined to carry back from Vietnam years later. It was a festering abscess of guilt and tortured thoughts that poisons the mind and eventually kills the soul unless it can be lanced and drained. Maybe that's one of the reasons my dad was so filled with anger. Maybe that's why he drank so much — to drown the painful memories that gnawed at his soul. Maybe that's the reason we both came home the way we did.

Sometimes he'd get knee-walkin' drunk and go into a blind rage, screaming threats at unseen enemies and vowing to kill anyone or anything that got in his way. My mom once told me that they found him one night at my granddaddy's farm lying in a snowbank, buck naked with a bottle of whiskey in one hand. He had been standing outside in the freezing cold, hurling threats and cursing the darkness.

My mom bore the brunt of his abuse — most of it verbal, some of it physical. She was a woman who spent much of her life suffering from his emotional tyranny. My dad would come home drunk, swearing and threatening to beat her. I loved my dad in spite of himself, but his abuse toward my mom wounded my heart deeply.

Like father like son, I soon inherited the sins of my father. My dad's character began to affect me at an early age. In his own twisted way he did his best to pass on the lessons he had learned in the "school of hard knocks." He didn't spend much time with me and didn't teach me much, but his example did wear off on me. The few things he did teach me were destined to set me on the path I eventually chose.

I was a pudgy little kid, who seemed to attract the attention of playground bullies. We'd move to a new town and I'd follow the well-worn ritual of setting off for school with my little lunch sack. I'd get to the playground and some juvenile thug would zero in on me like a wolf singling out a stray from the herd to pick a fight with me. It was like the punk gunslinger in the westerns who was always picking a fight with some poor cowhand so he could add another notch to his pistol and make a big name for himself. Many a day in elementary school I would come home with a busted lip or black eyes.

When I came home from school one day with a swollen lip, my daddy said, "I ain't gonna have any son of mine gettin' beat up all the time! Come on out in the garage, boy. Your dad is going to show you how to fight." I remember his looking down at me sternly and saying, "Listen, son, if there is one thing in my life I have learned, it's how to defend myself with my fists. I've been in enough fights to know."

One of the boxing pointers he gave me was to get in the first blow before my opponent had a chance to get me. It was kind of a perverted twist on the Golden Rule — "do unto others before they do unto you."

"From now on, son, when you go to a new school, I want you to find out who the toughest kid in your class is. When you do, I want you to walk up to him without his ever seeing what's coming and punch him as hard as you can in the face. You hear me? I want you to hit him as hard as you can in the nose. You might get into a good fight, and he may take you, but it will only be one fight and I guarantee from then on no one will mess with you anymore."

Well, being an obedient son, I followed my dad's instructions to the letter, and in no time I started getting a reputation as a tough guy who didn't take lip from anyone. Once, when we'd moved to Webster, Texas, some big eighth-grade boys were hassling some of us fourth graders on the school bus. They were trying to pull our pants down. My dad had told me that if I had to fight someone bigger than me anything was fair. When one of the boys grabbed me from behind and tried to get me in a headlock, I pried one of his little fingers up and bit it right off. The bus driver slammed on his brakes and threw me off of the bus. I never saw that boy again.

By the time I hit my teenage years I had already gained a reputation of being like James Dean in *Rebel Without a Cause*. I'd become every neighborhood's worst nightmare. I had already had several run-ins with the police and had been picked up several times for juvenile delinquency. When I was thirteen I was arrested, cuffed, and booked for unlawful possession of stolen explosives and was "popped" for stealing as well. At the rate I was going I was a prime candidate for Attica or San Quentin in a few years. My old man was seldom around, and my poor mom didn't know how to control me any longer.

Mom realized she'd lost control when the local sheriff pulled up to our house one day with the lights flashing and started toward the door with his police revolver drawn. I took one look out the door and bolted for the back window in an attempt to flee into the surrounding woods. I was halfway through the window when the cop burst through the front door shouting, "Stop, or I'll shoot!" My mother was crying and clinging to his sleeve screaming, "Don't shoot my boy; he's my only boy! Please don't kill my boy!"

He shouted again, "I mean it, boy. Go through that window and I'll shoot!"

I only got out of that tight spot through fast talking and some friends who knew a judge.

While I was growing up, my dad taught me the kind of things he thought would mold me into someone who could cope with the harsh realities this world would dish out — like how to fight dirty or shoot a gun, or like the time he showed me how to chew up double-edged razor blades and light bulbs and swallow them to intimidate my schoolmates. Maybe that was his crude way of preparing me for life the only way he knew how.

By the time I was sixteen I had been in more fights than I could remember. I had a bellyful of my father's aggression and could be more unpredictable than a cornered rattler. My aggression had also begun to reach an ominous level of brutality. It was no longer just enough to whip somebody in a fair fistfight; I wanted to draw blood. I wasn't content just to win a fight; I wanted to hurt my opponent and hurt him bad — like the time after high school just before my friend Len and I enlisted in the service — Len in the Marines and I in the Navy. We were driving home from school one afternoon when I saw a bully who had harassed us when we were younger. "Hey, Len, check it out!" I pointed up ahead to a guy walking toward us on the other side of the road. He was shuffling along carrying a sack slung over his shoulder. "Man, remember that guy, how he used to always torment us and chase us down when we were little? Man, that jerk was always picking on us. I told him I wasn't always going to be little, and one day I'd grow up and kick his rear. Pull over, Len, I'm going to give him a lesson he won't forget."

Len eased the car over to the grassy shoulder and pulled to a stop. I jumped out, looked both ways, and ran across the street. "Remember me, punk?" I asked as I ran up to the bully. He stopped dead in his tracks. I was smiling at the guy with a cocky expression on my face.

"No...no, I don't know who you are," he responded warily.

"Oh, yes, you do," I said. "You used to pick on me and my buddy when we were in junior high. Remember? Remember, I told you that I was going to grow up someday? Sucker, that day has come!" I said as I stepped toward him.

"I...I swear, I don't know you," he pleaded in a cowering voice as he backed up and stumbled.

I jumped him as he was going down and started beating him senseless. When I had beaten him unconscious I got up, brushed off my jeans, and walked across the road.

"What's wrong with him?" Len asked as I climbed into the front seat. "All I could see was your two fists going up and down like pistons."

"I left him lying in the ditch. I guess he was tired and wanted to catch a little sleep," I said sarcastically. Len busted out laughing and took off.

The next day his parents called my mom. The boy was taken to the hospital with a concussion, severe lacerations, and contusions on his head. When my mom hung up I could tell she was furious.

"What did you do to that boy, Mac?" she growled as she pointed her finger in my face.

"Aw, nothin' Mom. It was no big deal. I was just taking care of some old business."

She began to scream at me and give me a real tongue-lashing. "Why do you act this way? You ought to be ashamed of yourself. Why did you turn out like this?" she demanded.

"You outta know," I said contemptuously as I turned and walked out the door. It was the first time I had seen my mom mad, and one of the last times I saw her before I caught the Greyhound to Montgomery to join up on the "buddy system" with my friends Jimmy and Don.

Bustin' Bricks
• • •

It was about two in the morning. An ARVN inter-preter had accompanied me to my night ambush position concealed in thick stands of brush that rose like a lush green wall from the river's edge. We were just downstream from a cluster of sampans, basket boats, and rickety junks. They were moored to some narrow wooden foot piers jutting out from the bank. It was pre-dawn, when the mind begins to wander and the concentration dulls. I'd spent the last hour watching flares spiraling downward across the river under their tiny parachutes while they gave off a hissing corkscrew of smoke. The swaying flares bathed the river bottom in an eerie green glow that only added to the mesmer-izing feeling of that night hour.

The interpreter had accompanied me that night in the event we had to interrogate anyone. The river traffic had increased over the last few days, and with it, the number of pre-dawn sapper attacks along the Da Nang River. The "brass" were worried that the sappers might be preparing to hit the POL depot downriver where they stored large quantities of petroleum, oil, and lubricants to keep the Phantom jets flying on their constant bombing runs out of the busy Da Nang Air Base.

I was lying there with my M-14 against my shoulder watching the wooden shanties perched over the muddy flats on tall, spindly stilts silhouetted in the flare light across the river. The light show wavered in and out for a few minutes, then the curtain of blackness enveloped us again. Unknown to us, several boat loads of VC infiltrators had been waiting for the lights to go out before proceeding downstream. They had been camouflaged in the thick brush overhanging the opposite bank upstream.

I heard a sudden rustling of bushes near us. My heart started pumping adrenaline and I turned to fire toward the sound when this old gnarly papa sanh clawed his way through the brush shouting, "VC! VC! VC! Many VC Lai Dai! Come quickly! Many VC!" The weathered old face showed the strain of worry as he beckoned me excitedly. His teeth were rotted and blackened from years of chewing betel nut and his breath reeked of fish sauce and decay.

I instructed the ARVN interpreter to head downriver to get reinforcements and followed the old pajama-clad man upstream to intercept the VC coming toward us. We scurried through the tangled vegetation until we reached an area overlooking a wide spot in the river where I could faintly make out a cluster of shallow sampans floating downstream. I raised my rifle to my shoulder, flicked the selector switch to fully automatic and fired off a burst that kicked up geysers of water all around the lead boat. I then quickly scrambled to a new position and fired off another burst. I was trying to make it seem like there were more of us than just the old papa sanh and me. I was running through the foliage to a new position when muzzle flashes flickered from one of the sampans and rounds splatted into the muddy bank around me, blowing chunks of mud and vegetation from the ground.

I scanned the river bottom and saw the trailing sampans veering off toward the opposite bank farther downstream. The lead boat had been cut off from the others and was drifting close to the sampans moored on my side of the bank. I heard a splash and saw one of the VC swimming toward them to escape. I couldn't shoot anymore toward the sampans because they had drifted directly across from the Third MAF camp and I ran the risk of hitting some of our own guys if I opened up. The VC were smart.

The old man and I maneuvered toward the cluster of junks and sampans to capture the fleeing VC. Adrenaline was rushing through my system. My heart was pounding out of my chest. It was him or me as we closed in. The old man was just as determined to get the lone VC. We began to grope our way through the brush on the river's edge, moving closer to the waiting sampans. I started shouting out, "VC, Lai Dai, Lai Dai!" With all the racket I was making, I was waking up the fishing families who lived on the boats. I could hear them swearing at me in Vietnamese. We climbed over the boats, kicking over anything the VC could have been hiding under. The old guy stayed by my side and covered my back. We were like two bloodhounds closing in for the kill. I wasn't bothering to check I.D.'s because there was no time to waste as we climbed from boat to boat. The old man went over the side, into that filthy water, and started groping along the bottoms and the sides of the hulls in an attempt to locate the hiding man. I was scared out of my wits, expecting the flash of a rifle barrel in my face or the sudden lunge of a knife blade. I followed the bubbles of the old man as he swam between the boats looking for the VC who might have been hiding underwater and breathing through a reed.

We kept up our search until the violet half-tones and apricot hues of dawn began to blush in the east. We never found the guy. He must have slipped away in the darkness and melted back into the sanctuary of the jungle. It was another night locked in an electric chair of nerve-fraying suspense — another night where I had come dangerously close to the lethal edge once again.

Several months of night ambushes with my one-man killer team had left me coiled tighter than a steel spring. I was hitting the booze at the local brothels on my off-duty hours to numb my nerves and find a temporary release from the strain. When I wasn't in the pressure cooker you could find me hunkered down at one of the raunchy hangouts suckin' suds or hustlin' bar girls.

One afternoon early in my tour I was driving across the Da Nang Bridge heading for a compound at the base of "Monkey Mountain" to pick up some supplies when I passed a guy in civilian clothes thumbing a ride beside the road. I eased the big deuce-and-a-half over to the shoulder and let the guy catch up with me.

"Need a lift?" I said as the man climbed up on the running board and gave me a toothy grin through the window. He was Oriental and looked like he was in his thirties.

"Can you give me a ride into Da Nang, prease?" he asked.

"No sweat-tee-da, man. Climb on in," I responded.

I eased the pedal down and pulled back onto the road with a grind of gears and the throaty belch of the diesel engine.

"My name John Young Koo." He smiled and extended his hand.

I reached over to shake it, trying to keep my eye on the road as we negotiated a throng of Vespas, bicycles, and Vietnamese pedestrians hauling goods to the marketplace.

I looked over at the little man bouncing up and down on the seat and said, "You'd better keep your head down, buddy, 'cause we get sniper fire through this stretch once in a while. Sometimes the gooks, I mean the Vietnamese, throw junk at us. Last week one kid threw a Coke bottle at me. If we get hit we may have to pull this rig over and jump in the ditch."

"I not afraid," he said matter-of-factly.

I asked him how long he had been in-country. He said that he had been there for a few months training his countrymen in special jungle survival tactics, but was now doing business for some company in Korea and was planning on staying for three years. When he told me that he had been with the famous Korean "Fighting Tigers" I knew he wasn't your ordinary humble Oriental. The "ROKs," the Republic of Korean Marines, had a fierce reputation. They were about as ruthless and dedicated as they come. The VC feared them so much that they tried to stay clear of any areas the ROKs were operating in. The ROKs had quite a reputation for showing the enemy no mercy.

I remember glancing over at him again and seeing this little man, maybe four-foot-eleven at the most, sitting there serenely with his hands folded on his lap just swaying with the movement of the cab — as calm as could be.

That's when I noticed that his hand looked deformed or swollen. One of his knuckles was enlarged like it had just been broken.

"Aw, man, how did ya hurt your hand?" I asked.

"What yo mean?" he responded, not understanding what I meant.

"Your hand, man. It looks like you really messed it up," I said as I pointed to his knuckle.

"Aw, no hurt. Karate knuckle," he laughed. "Stop truck, stop truck," he urged.

We were kind of on the outskirts of town with nothing much around so I eased the truck off the roadway, even though I didn't like stopping.

John walked over to a pile of bricks he had eyed lying next to a low stuccoed wall and picked one up.

"You see," he said as he instructed me to hold the brick out in front of me with both hands. "KeeYah!" he snapped as he drove his knuckle into the brick, shattering it into pieces.

"Wow, man, that's far out," I shouted. I couldn't believe this little guy could do something like that with such ease.

"That doesn't hurt?" I asked in amazement.

"No, no — no, hurt," he assured me.

"How did ya do that?" I wondered.

"Not size of man that is important," John smiled, "but discipline and concentration. Friends call me 'Little John.' Ha, ha, ha," he doubled over in laughter.

"Man, I wish I could do that," I shrugged.

"You want learn karate?" he responded. "John Young Koo teach you!"

"Hey, John, can you come back with me to my base and show some of the guys what you can do?" I asked.

"No problem! Can do," he said. "We start karate school, okay?" he added.

"Man, that would be outta sight," I replied.

Later that afternoon, we arrived at my compound and I introduced John to the rest of the guys. I gathered as many as I could find and they crowded around John for the karate demonstration. Needless to say, they were as blown away as I had been when he disintegrated another brick with one precise blow. After he showed us how effective karate could be, some of us got to work organizing a karate school. In no time we were holding classes six days a week, three to four hours a session. I spent every spare moment I could find under John's personal instruction. I'd been pretty good with my fists for a long time, but this was a whole new art of fighting I was eager to learn.

John took me under his wing and started grooming me and teaching me some of his personal secrets and tricks of the trade to really be effective. My skills developed quickly because he poured so much time into personally training me.

I remember his telling me that many people try to teach the various forms of karate, but he said, "What good is a fruit tree if it does not bear fruit?" Generally, the students learn the motions, but learn nothing more than a beautiful dance — useless as a real weapon in a life-or-death situation. So he really pushed us. Because of the punishing intensity of the off-duty training most lost interest and dropped out, but a few of us hung in there.

About a week after our training had begun, John brought me a large brick wound tightly with hard hemp cord. "Mac, I want you hit this brick many times a day — at least a thousand times. Understand?" He looked me sternly in the face.

"Yes," I accepted the assignment without questioning.

"You will experience pain at first...then knuckle will break. When this happens you will only rest for a while...then you must begin to strike the brick again. In time, skin will get hard and calloused, but knuckle will grow because calcium will grow over it and will one day become like mine," he said as he held his knuckle up.

I followed his instructions and in several weeks I had broken my knuckle three times, but the skin became as tough as a rhinoceros's hide. It no longer cracked or broke open.

After a couple months of rigorous training John got permission from our CO to take some of us out in the bush to give demonstrations to Marine units stationed at fighting bases on some of the strategic hills south of Da Nang in Que Son Valley —like Hill 55 and 63. He wanted us to show the Marines how much more effective they could be if they knew how to use this form of karate.

He also started to organize karate matches and even got some judges to come from Korea to judge the matches. I advanced quickly and won all of my matches.

The one thing that the art of karate taught me was concentration and control. I had been fighting for years, but the disciplines of karate were a far cry from the slugfests I had experienced growing up. John taught me to focus my energies and conserve my strength — to use my blows sparingly, powerfully, but effectively. How unlike the crude free-for-alls I had known in high school, flailing away at my opponent, punching his face again and again like a berserk pile-driver. My fighting skills had become a deadly art form — a ballet of timing and movement. They were not like the hockey riots I had known so often in high school when I was seriously beating my opponents (like the time in the cafeteria when a brawl broke out and I silenced one loudmouth senior by punching his face in so brutally I knocked an eye out of its socket and left him blind in one eye, or the time in the locker room when I mauled another kid, bashing his head against the concrete floor so badly I turned his face into a bloody pulp, spattering his blood all over the lockers and pooling it on the floor). For a brief season during the middle of my tour I experienced a measure of discipline and control, but my instability would soon ensure its end.

After a few months the discipline I learned began to evaporate in the heat and hostility of Nam. The control and restraint that John Young Koo had begun to cultivate in me were soon destroyed by the turbulent undercurrents tugging at my heart, undercurrents of unrest that had been undermining me from my childhood.

It wasn't long before I began to waste my training in destructive outlets. When I wasn't pulling night ambush or sharpening my training under John Koo I was unwinding at one of the favorite drinking holes I frequented. At one of the bars there was a ring in back with a boxing match going on between anyone who wanted to mix it up. A couple of my buddies encouraged me to get in the ring and see if I could beat a burley

Marine who was taunting the crowd. Mastery of the ring was held by the man who could stay on his feet and eliminate any and all comers. The Marine was a big barrelchested guy with a faded tattoo of a Marine Corps emblem on one arm and a bulldog on the other. He'd already knocked out a civilian construction worker, a Seabee, and a couple of squids, and was threatening to "mop the floor with any swabby stupid enough to climb into the ring with him." According to him, he was the baddest mother on earth. Well, I had never liked bullies and the coaxing of my drunken buddies was all it took.

I promptly climbed through the ropes and beat the livin' daylights out of him. With a lightning flurry of blows I cold-cocked him so hard he was out for half an hour. It was over in the first round. I had gotten pretty good with my fists, but the combination of speed and agility gained from my karate training was devastating. Needless to say, the crowd of rowdy onlookers was quite impressed.

It wasn't long before I started gaining a reputation for being a real tough fighter. The guys in the bar would come up to me after a fight and say, "Hey, man, look at your big baby face; you don't have a scratch on it!" They started calling me Cassius Clay and Muhammad Ali and making up rhymes and jiving me about how bad I was. I began to thrive on the excitement and really got off on the praise.

But the excitement and novelty gradually grew old. The excitement and adulation of the crowd were a nice reprieve from the constant demands of my night ambushes, but the relentless pressures eventually ground me down and sucked the enthusiasm out of me until I had no more energy left to give. I began to retreat more and more into myself and the numbing escape of alcohol.

Dustoff

• • •

The warm blast of kerosene fumes and the buffeting downdraft of the slowly spinning blades whipped the air as the corpsmen carried my litter into the receiving station at the Ninety-seventh Evac Hospital in Da Nang. The relentless *Dhup, Dhup, Dhup* of incoming Hueys signaled the arrival of more dustoffs from the field.

The next few moments are indelibly etched in my mind. The scene was one of absolute chaos as they carried me through the doors. Partially clad Marines littered the floor. Others were sprawled across wooden receiving tables scattered with stainless steel trays and surgical instruments. Some were tethered with rubber tubing to plasma bags and saline bottles. Some were writhing in agony, others were screaming for more morphine, while others were simply crying.

The receiving room looked like a slaughterhouse. I had arrived just as a covey of medevacs were landing with casualties from a fire fight to deposit their human cargo of wounded and dying. The interior of the room was a grisly portfolio of snapshots. It was a sickening world of audible and visual horrors I will never forget. Teenage Marines had been carried in with sucking chest wounds frothing with tiny pink bubbles, shredded stumps from traumatic amputations, and muddy fatigues stained blood-black from the hemorrhaging wounds of high-velocity rounds. Along one wall was an olive-drab stretcher piled with a mound of anonymous body parts. Soiled field dressings and discarded bandages littered the floor. The nauseating stench of body fluids, paddy funk, and sour sweat filled the room.

The shock of that naked carnage was devastating. It was everything I could do to choke back the bile rising in my throat. But the sickening feeling of guilt was even more overpowering. Yeah, I'd spent endless nights alone in the jungle waiting for Charlie to appear. Yeah, I'd risked my life in an expendable situation for months on end, but what was that in comparison to the sight of those dead and dying? I was only suffering from an acute case of dysentery and fatigue, being carried past men who had been slopping through rice paddies and thick jungles fighting North Vietnamese regulars head-on. The confrontation tore me apart with guilt — guilt for not having done more, guilt that someone else was laying down his life, guilt that I hadn't paid my dues, guilt that I had not suffered more, guilt that I wasn't one of them bleeding on the floor.

Like most adolescent soldiers, I shipped out to Vietnam with a head filled with romantic notions of combat. I was pretty "gungho" and had boasted along with my fellow warriors of how many "gooks" we were going to grease or how many "Cong" we were going to kill. But, in short order, each of us was introduced to the bestial insanities of war and confusing contradictions of Vietnam.

I had volunteered for the Navy and followed the time-honored rituals of countless recruits. I had endured the indignities of the preinduction physical, shuffling like mindless robots down endless corridors in our hospital gowns and paper slippers following a maze of pastel paths painted on linoleum floors. My herd of adolescents had been subjected to a humiliating battery of bending, coughing, spreading, poking, and urinating. I remember the matter-of-fact indifference of the physicians who examined us. We had endured this dehumanizing ritual, feeling more like cattle being processed through a stockyard than human beings with names and feelings. Along the way some had been eliminated as "4-F" because of flat feet, perforated eardrums, color blindness, high blood pressure, asthma, poor hearing, bad eyes, bad blood, and bad urine. Some took it hard, while others received the news as if they had just won the Irish Sweepstakes. I had progressed down the little painted trails from one exam station to the next until I completed them all — relieved that I had passed with a 1-A classification and not been mustered out.

Like multitudes before me, I had been deposited in the early-morning twilight at the Naval Training Depot in San Diego after an exhausting flight from Alabama. The long trip had left me burnt out and disoriented — just the zombie-like state designed by Pentagon minds as the first stage of a well-thought-out program of dehumanization and loss of identity. We were no longer human beings, but pukes, slime, maggots, queers, and every vile thing known to man. On the evolutionary charts we ranked alongside jellyfish and slugs. For the next two months of shots, PT, classrooms, and obstacle courses we were subjected to a daily bombardment of obscene characterizations and profane putdowns, which would make a veteran longshoreman wince.

After the rigors of boot-camp I was stationed at Seal Island, seventy-two miles off the coast of Oxnard, where I was assigned to a special unit that worked out of Coronado to undergo underwater and special weapons training. While there, a couple of gnarly old "salts" took it upon themselves to do their Navy best to obliterate any last vestiges of youthful innocence by introducing me to Sodom and Gomorrah South — a.k.a. Tijuana. That's where I experienced my initiation into the sordid nightlife of Tijuana's ten-dollar whores, raunchy bars, brawls, and weekend drunks — drinking so much tequila that I'd spend Monday mornings hugging a toilet bowl, puking my guts out.

When I finally boarded the long trans-Pacific flight, I flew toward Vietnam, ready to follow in the glorious footsteps of John Wayne and Audie Murphy. But, in spite of patriotic notions of guns, guts, and glory, I would soon learn that the celluloid portrayals every Tuesday night of Sergeant Striker and *The Sands of Iwo Jima* or Vic Morrow in "Combat" victoriously fighting his way across France every Tuesday night were sanitized versions of war, far removed from the naked perversities of the real thing.

I made the long, grueling flight across the Pacific with a small group of men who had trained together at Coronado. We were all pumped and ready for action, even though each of us sat in the dim confines of that transport in private inventory of our personal manhood. No one said it out loud, but every one of us was asking himself the same questions: "How will I react to this test? Will I prove to be a coward? Will I run the first time

I'm shot at? Do I have what it takes? Will I make it back in one piece?" The moment of truth had finally arrived. There was no turning back. We weren't going to be playing soldier from now on. The war games were over. The bullets were real. As I scanned the anxious faces of my fellow soldiers, I asked myself, "How many of us will make the return flight a year from now? How many of us will go home early without arms or legs? How many will be going home in a box? How many will die in spirit?" It was a raucous flight until we reached Wake Island for refueling. The small talk and jovial banter of adolescent soldiers tapered off as we approached the coast of the Republic of Vietnam for our final descent. The atmosphere suddenly cooled as each of us braced himself for the unknown of the purgatory we were about to enter. Everyone tensed when the announcement came over the speaker that we would be landing shortly.

"This is it!" I thought to myself. "This is what I have trained for all these months!" I could hear the hydraulic whine of the landing gear coming down and the buffeting of the plane as the pilot adjusted the flaps to slow our descent. Just then the engines began to roar. The giant jet suddenly veered to the left and fought for altitude. A wave of adrenaline shot through the cabin as men looked at each other with fear on their faces.

Men flinched and squirmed around in the claustro-phobic confines of that cavernous cabin as stray rounds punctured the fuselage. All the John Wayne machismo suddenly evaporated in the heat of that moment. I was suddenly seized with the sickening fear that I had made a terrible mistake. A belly load of "new guys" all exhibited the same look of wide-eyed terror. The pilot came on the intercom and announced that we had taken some ground fire on our approach and we were going to have to hold in a circling pattern until the Marines could sweep the perimeter. Guys were really sweating it out for the next forty-five minutes while the jet circled the airfield. Men were pulling snapshots out of their wallets and looking at the wives, sweethearts, and families they left behind. Each was thinking that he might never see his loved ones again. I was wondering the same thing.

Like most, my whole introduction to Nam was a rude awakening. It came when I emerged from the air-conditioned comfort of our C-141 transport and stepped into the equatorial hell of that Vietnam night. No sooner had I stepped out into the night than I was soaked in perspiration. My senses were assaulted by the pungent stench of petroleum products, jet exhaust, rusting metal, Oriental cooking, spent ordinance, and human waste. They were the first steps in a long journey of disillusionment and pain.

I remember being herded from the transport with a heavy feeling in my gut as I scanned the sprawling air base. The twinkling lights in the velvet blackness had an eerie brooding quality that seemed to remind me how alone I felt and how far away from home I was. The distant sight on the horizon of a lone gunship hosing down the perimeter with a scarlet stream of tracer fire also reminded me that many unseen dangers lurked in the darkness I had stepped into.

I arrived that sweltering night in Da Nang unsure of what to expect. But the sobering realities of Vietnam steadily ground me down. Since I had received special weapons training at Coronado, I was assigned to work with the Third MAF (Marine Amphibious Force) with the responsibility of night ambushes — interdicting river-borne sappers and infiltrators who threatened to sabotage the many fuel depots and storage facilities along the bustling Da Nang river. Though I had enlisted in the Navy, I worked with the Marines during my tour in Nam.

My job was one of stealth and cunning. I was a night predator who played a deadly game of hide-and-seek with the enemy, lurking on the banks of one of the Viet Cong's key infiltration routes into the Da Nang Seaport. At night, I would be escorted by a Marine patrol to a prearranged location where I quietly fell out of the squad and slipped into the camouflaged concealment of the secluded spot along the river to watch and wait.

I was green at first, but the demands of night ambush quickly honed my skills. My job required that I learn the fine art of staying alive. I steadily mastered the skills of surviving on the lethal edge. Night vision, a sharpness of sight, peripheral vision, and a keen sixth sense, were some of the ambient skills you had to learn if you wanted to stay alive stalking Charlie at night. Night ambush was a game whose outcome depended upon every muscle, every sinew, every nerve ending being alert and poised for action. It was a game of raw nerves that kept my system charged with adrenaline and constantly on edge.

Most of the time we didn't know who our enemy was. By day he could be one of the local farmers plowing his rice paddies in time-honored fashion behind his water buffalo, working in the PX, or shaving your neck with a straight razor in the barber shop. At night that same person could be booby-trapping a trail with homemade explosives. By day she could be the compound's laundry woman walking off distances for mortar attacks or the smiling shoeshine boy eavesdropping on GI scuttlebutt.

Vietnam had no fronts. It was a war against an elusive and tenacious enemy who often wore little more than black pajamas and Ho Chi Minh sandals and could live on a handful of rice a day. The night belonged to him and he was as resourceful and cunning as they come. We quickly learned that any one of the Vietnamese could be the enemy — from the little kid selling Coke to the delicate young woman carrying a basketful of fruit. They could be everywhere and nowhere at the same time. You just never knew for sure, so you stayed on edge and never let your guard down. You soon learned to live in a heightened state of nerve-fraying suspense.

Most of the time it was a war of nerves — of endless stretches of mind-numbing monotony or backbreaking exhaustion. It was a black-and-white war of boredom and drudgery, which was only occasionally punctuated by the technicolor terror of a fire fight, tripped booby trap, or incoming fire. It was an emotional roller coaster that fluctuated between monotony and high-intensity terror. It was a "wait and see" war of nerves that took a steady toll on men's minds and emotions.

Many a night I spent hunkered down behind the lush curtains of jungle greens — sweating out the night, as tense as a time bomb. Those nights along the Da Nang River had many faces. I spent many apprehensive nights in ominous solitude waiting and hoping for the dawn. There were vulnerable nights lurking in a clump of brush waiting for a VC sampan to drift past. There were noisy nights listening to the ebb and flow of river traffic plying the water way. There were routine nights when the repeated shouts of "Lai Dai, Lai Dai" (Come here, come here) earned little more than a flurry of curses from angry fishermen who would kick the dirt and gutturally denounce us with the typical "GI number ten, GI no good, no care for our country. GI filthy stinking pigs!" There were oppressive foreboding nights when you could sense the enemy's closeness. There were anxious nights of anticipation, waiting for a river shootout that would never come. There were nights so black that you couldn't see your hand in front of your face. There were eerie brooding nights faintly lit by the yellow tint of moonlight; quiet nights when the luminous silhouette of clouds drifted beneath a full moon; distant, velvet nights of endless stars.

Most were long, tedious nights that weighed heavily upon my mind. They were clammy, restless nights, with a round chambered in my M-14 and my finger impatiently caressing the trigger, secretly hoping the enemy would show so the boredom could be broken. And there were nights of high-intensity terror when the shouts to stop would be answered with the distinctive crack of AKs and the river would suddenly be thrown into upheaval by the blast of a mine.

Besides the boredom and suspense and isolation, night ambushes could be a world of physical discomfort and misery. The demand for quietness required sitting motionless in one position for hours on end. Unnecessary movement had to be avoided to lessen the chances of noise — especially along the river where sounds could carry for long distances. Many a night I had to endure the incessant whine of attacking mosquitoes or the constant ratcheting of insects. Slapping your neck or groping for leeches could be lethal.

Many a night during the dry season it would get so hot and humid it was nearly suffocating. The air would be so saturated with moisture it was like breathing inside a plastic bag. You sweated like water pouring through a sieve in that jungle sauna. Streams of perspiration would course through oily insect repellent and jungle grime, stinging eyes and blurring vision. On torrid nights like that it seemed like I was being slowly strangled by a living force — like the vegetation was actually closing in around me.

By the time I found myself at the Ninety-seventh Evac I had spent months on night ambush along the Da Nang River. My night ambush experience had earned me a temporary assignment guarding a South Vietnamese colonel the Viet Cong had put a contract out on. After three weeks of six hours on, six hours off, around-the-clock guarding of his villa on the outskirts of Da Nang, I collapsed from sleep deprivation and exhaustion. A bad case of the "Saigon Shuffle" hadn't helped. The constant pressures of night watches and diarrhea had beaten me down.

Some delicate inner mechanism that had been wound too tight for too long had suddenly snapped. The scene of carnage in that hospital had pushed me over the edge. After two weeks I was released and returned to my unit. But I wasn't the same. During the last remaining months of my tour, I started retreating ever deeper into myself and even abandoned the few drinking buddies I had. I was drinking more and taking foolish chances, unconsciously playing out a secret "death wish" to somehow atone for the overwhelming burden of guilt that gnawed at my insides like a cancer.

Jungle Nights

• • •

It was one of those hot, sweltering nights I'd learned to hate so much — one of those hot, sticky nights at the beginning of the dry season when the countryside sweated itself free of billions of gallons of moisture left behind by the monsoon rains. The fourteen-man patrol completed its pre-dawn mission and was returning to our compound with the three night ambushers they had dropped off the evening before. I was the last man to be retrieved.

It had been a melancholy night of dark thoughts and bitter reflections. The solitude of my jungle hideaways gave me plenty of opportunities to think. A week before, a new guy had died in my hooch and his body had been unceremoniously sent to the morgue unit in Da Nang for shipment back home. The incident left me bitter and angry.

I had taken a liking to the kid, even though he was what we sarcastically referred to as a "cherry." He was about as green as they come. He was a baby-faced teenager, scared spitless. The night flares, muffled explosions, and tracer fire from gunships probing suspected VC locations in the surrounding hills had really shaken him. I was drawn to the kid and felt sorry for him — maybe because I knew how bad it felt to be alone and scared myself. He was drawn to me like a cowering puppy, but all my reassuring did little to comfort his fears.

Two weeks after his arrival in-country he came down with a high temperature. He was burning up. I stayed up all night with him trying to cool him down with wet towels, but he kept shaking and sweating. In the morning I helped him over to the aid station and begged the two corpsmen to send him to the hospital in Da Nang, but they just laughed and shrugged it off as no big deal. They gave him a shot and said he'd be fine, but he wasn't fine — a blind man could see that. I pleaded with them to send him to the hospital, but they were indifferent.

The next morning I found his body lying in his bunk, stiff and cold. Like many in Vietnam, he had died in the darkness from indifference and neglect — just another cold statistic.

I really lost it. I started screaming and cursing and vowed to kill those meatheads who let the kid die needlessly. I was kicking over bunks and tearing things from the wall. It took several guys to hold me down. I mean I went berserk — completely flipped out.

It wasn't enough that they'd hung me out on a line night after night to dry, that they'd cut me off and dumped me alone in a potential killing zone like a worm on a hook. The system had callously let that innocent kid just die. They'd discarded him like a piece of worthless garbage, then zipped him up in that body bag and shipped him home like it was just part of the routine.

Everything had become such a waste. The bitterness and disillusionment that had been gnawing at my gut for years had reached a new intensity.

That morning, when I came unglued, I finally reached such a point of bitterness and anger that, for the first time, I wanted to kill. Seeing the scared look on the faces of those guys trying to restrain me that morning made me flash back to the time when the tables had been turned and my dad had nearly killed me in a blind flash of rage.

The constant fighting between my mom and dad had become unbearable. I had lain in my bed countless nights with the pillow crammed over my ears to shut out the screaming and swearing. It seemed like all they cared about was themselves and their own miserable lives. The anger and hatred in our home was reaching a flashpoint and I was afraid my daddy was going to come home drunk one night and beat my mom to death in a rage.

I remember getting in his face one night and telling him, "When I reach sixteen, you'll never hurt my mom again." I'd warned him to leave her alone, but they'd just get into another "knock down, drag out" fight and he'd slam the door and head to the nearest bar.

I was nearly sixteen when it happened. I was big and muscular. Two years of varsity football and raising hell had left me muscular and mean. I had been a dismal student, but the one thing I was good at in high school was football— maybe because the clash at the scrimmage line fit my mentality. My success as a left guard had boosted my self-confidence and prepared me for the inevitable showdown with my dad.

When I finally reached sixteen the day of confrontation arrived. I had just walked outside with my friend Glenn when I heard my dad's car pull up out in front. I saw him get out of the car with another guy and start for the house. He walked up to me and said, "Where's your mama, boy?"

"I don't know, but you're not coming in this house!" I said as I pointed my finger in his face. "You're not going to hit my mother anymore," I warned. By that time I weighed a muscular two hundred pounds, so I figured I could take my dad. But I forgot how lean and mean he really was.

"Get outta my way, you little..." He growled as he took a step toward me.

"You're not coming in!" I shouted.

He screamed as he lunged for me. We were wrestling with each other, when he finally tripped me and threw me to the ground. We were struggling and flailing with our arms and legs. Each was trying to gain the upper hand, but he was faster and stronger. He grabbed me around the neck, locking his hands around my throat, and started squeezing with all his strength. I was choking and gasping for air, trying to pry his hands off. I was losing strength and starting to black out. I remember looking at his beet-red face, seeing him gritting his teeth and looking at me with those murderous eyes while he choked me and banged my head against the grass. He had a demented grin on his face I will never forget. Finally my face began to turn purple. My friend was screaming, "Stop, Mr. Gober, you're killing him! Please stop!" That's when his drinking buddy said, "C'mon, Bill, let's go. The kid's not worth it! Hell, he's not even a man. He's learned his lesson." My dad finally let go, cursed, then got up and left.

That was one of the last times I saw my dad before I enlisted. I think I came pretty close to hating him at that moment — not just for trying to kill me, but for a lifetime of abuse and neglect. I thought that I would care less if I ever saw him again. But a few months later, after not hearing a word from him — not a letter or phone call — I realized that I still hadn't shut him out completely. Even when I got to Nam I would go to mail-call secretly hoping I'd get a letter from home with just a few words from my dad. I got letters and "care" packages from my high school sweetheart like clockwork, but not a single letter from my dad, and I really resented him for that. It was one thing that he hadn't cared enough to come to any of my football games or show the least concern about my school work, but not to show that he cared for me when I was risking my life overseas was especially galling. It didn't make any sense to me, especially when he had known firsthand what it was like to face the fears and perversities of war. At least he could have written one letter.

After so many painful years of rejection, I was still clinging to a shred of hope that things could be right with us. I guess, deep down inside, I was still clinging to the hope that my dad would love me and show me that he cared for me and my mom. I had wanted that from my earliest memories.

I remember how much I had yearned for my dad's affection when I was a little boy. I had loved him with a child's simple love and had cried late into the night, asking my mom where dad was after weeks of absence. When we weren't drifting from Hamburg, to Little

Rock, to Mobile, to Pine Bluff, we were waiting for Dad to come home from some construction site in another town. Many nights I'd cry in my mom's arms asking, "Mamma, why don't Daddy come home? Doesn't he love us anymore?" My mom would just hold me tight and soothe my tears as best she could.

On many occasions when I was little I would be playing in the yard with beer cans, pushing them around the dirt. I would look up hoping I would see my dad coming home. I would go down to the corner to watch and wait for my dad's '49 Ford to come around the corner. Day after day would pass before I'd see his old beat-up Ford and my heart would leap with joy. I remember running beside his car in my bare feet shouting with glee, "Daddy! Daddy!" He would drive past the house and just keep on going down the street with me running after him. I'd run until I was exhausted, then finally give up, turn around, and plod back crying to our house. I couldn't understand why he wouldn't slow down and play with me. And I remember the time when I finally caught up with his car, parked in a vacant lot down the street, and found him slumped over the steering wheel in a drunken stupor.

I remember begging my dad to stop drinking. He would always lie about it or make up some lame excuse to cover his alcoholism. He'd come home with a strawberry cola can, and I'd think my dad wasn't drinking anymore. He'd set it down and I'd smell it. It would stink of warm beer or whiskey. He'd try to gloss over his drinking and lying by making promises he never kept — "We'll go here!" "Your dad's going to do this with you." None of his promises of taking me fishing or hunting ever came true. It hurt me. I put so much stock in what my dad said, but it was all just empty lies. My dad's promises kept me full of hope for a season, then I began to realize that he didn't mean any of them. I began to grow bitter. The root of bitterness, which took hold of my heart more and more as I grew up, grew from the seeds my dad had sown so early in my life.

Oh, he showed me how to fight and shoot a gun and stand up for myself, but he seldom showed me he cared. He'd drag me around with his drinking buddies to the local road-houses and bars in his version of a "father and son outing," but he cared more for his booze and sleazy pickups than for me. Still, I loved my dad, in spite of himself, and wanted a closeness with him I had never known. It is one of the cruel testaments to a child's love for his parents. Even children who have been beaten and abused and burned with cigarette butts or scalded with boiling water still long for their parents' acceptance and yearn for their love. Maybe that's why, in spite of the constant abuse and tension, I was still torn to pieces when my mom wrote me in boot camp and informed me that she and my dad were getting a divorce.

The few times I can remember as a little guy when my dad and I shared anything close to a normal father and son relationship were when he would lift me up onto the seat of his Indian motorcycle. The cycle looked just like one of those old flathead Harley Davidsons with the side shifts. I still have a picture of my dad and me sitting on that old thing. The highlights of my childhood were the times when my old man would put me up on that cycle and take me for a spin down the back roads of Texas.

Our pre-dawn patrol filed into our compound that morning in the violet half-light in a brooding frame of mind. A heaviness settled upon me that I couldn't shake. As we approached the guards at the gate to give our passwords and I.D. checks, I could tell they were acting a little weird.

"Hey, Mason, what gives, man?" the squad leader asked. It was obvious to all of us that something wasn't right. His usual bloodshot eyes had a tenseness we had never seen before.

"The stuff has hit the fan, that's what," he answered.

"What d'ya mean?" I asked, not sure what he was getting at. I was thinking in the back of my mind that some Viet Cong sappers had probably hit the compound the night before.

The rest of the squad gathered around out of curiosity.

"Looks like the blacks and whites done declared war," he replied as he clutched his weapon tightly. "The brothers jumped some white guys comin' out of the EM club last night and cut 'em up real bad. Three of our guys were knifed and two were shot. I mean, they beat the dog outta them and now it's our turn," Mason threatened in a menacing tone as he glared at a black Marine listening in.

"There it is!" a white Marine spit out the words.

"You got that right," another white Marine grunted.

"From now on, it's us against them," he added.

I couldn't believe it. It wasn't enough for Charlie to be sneaking around the countryside trying to kill us, but now the blacks wanted blood? News of racial tension, riots, and the black power thing back home hit like a hurricane, stirring up a hornet's nest of rage.

"Aw, man, this is too much. I don't believe this!" I responded. "It's not enough that long-haired freaks are burnin' the flag back home and praising Ho Chi Minh. It's not enough that the gooks are tryin' to kill us or rip us off every chance they get, but now we're starting to shoot each other?" I demanded as I walked off to my hooch.

From that point on the tension in the ranks was so thick you could cut it with a knife. Everyone lived in constant fear of being shot at or "fragged" in his bunk at night. The whole compound felt like a time bomb waiting to go off. No one went anywhere alone. It was the blacks versus the whites. Everyone carried his weapon — locked and loaded. The blacks hung out in their groups, and the whites hung out in theirs.

From that point on I retreated into a private world of hate and loneliness. Something had dried up and died inside me. The hardening process, fueled by nineteen years of hurt and hate, had turned me as cold as steel. From that point on I pulled back from the few friends that I had left. I put on an emotional flak jacket that shut everyone out. The seclusion and solitude of the jungle became my sanctuary. My only companion was the bottle, and I tried to stay as drunk as I could to numb the hurt.

It was the end of the line for me. I had finally given up. If no one cared back home, why should I? It was either me or them, so I chose me. I didn't want to be sacrificed for nothing. I was fed up with everything. I just wanted out. Even though I didn't have much of a family to go home to, I knew I didn't want to die in Vietnam, so I counted off the days on my "short-timer" calendar and stayed drunk most of the time, not giving a flip. Anyway, what could they do, send me to Vietnam?

Freedom Bird

•••

The time finally arrived when I had colored down the last day on my calendar girl and completed my tour in Vietnam. I'd struggled through the last few weeks in a daze. The combination of short-timer's fever and booze kept me in a haze.

On my last night I was stuffing my sea bag and squaring away my gear when some of the guys came over to wish me luck. There were some handshakes, backslaps, and some awkward words exchanged and then it was over. John Young Koo dropped by, too, and wished me prosperity and happiness. He said he hoped we would meet again. I hadn't seen him too much during the last couple of months, but I could tell by the look in his eye that he was going to miss me.

Now that the moment had come, I really couldn't believe that I was going home. I was finally catching the "freedom bird" back to the "land of the big PX." When I got to the airfield at Da Nang I was stunned when they marched us across the tarmac to a waiting commercial 727. It was one of those Braniffs, painted in psychedelic colors. I was even more stunned by the stewardesses who greeted us. They were the first round-eyed women I'd seen in a long time. It was all so unreal and yet so very real at the same time.

Like I said, when we entered the plane I was dumbfounded by the sight of the gorgeous round-eyed stewardesses. I sat down in a window seat and fastened my seat belt for the long journey home. In a few moments the jet taxied to takeoff, raced down the runway, and climbed steeply into a brilliant blue sky. I remember staring at the tops of the heads of the men in front of me in quiet contemplation. I was torn up inside — filled with all kinds of conflicting emotions. I couldn't stop replaying the things that had happened to me in Nam. When I had been cleaning out my footlocker and stuffing my gear into my sea bag the night before, I thought to myself that it was odd that I was carrying home less than when I first arrived, but that was only on the outside. Inside, my heart was heavy with a baggage full of hate and bitterness and depression.

The plane was strangely quiet at first. All you could hear was the steady whine of the jet engines as we gained altitude and climbed toward the South China Sea. Most of the men were sitting rigidly in their seats, secretly hoping and praying that they would get off the ground safely and not be shot at or somehow forced to return. Like me, they only half believed they were really going home. But as soon as the shout "feet wet" was heard, the plane exploded with a thunderous cheer and calls for the stewardesses to "bring on the drinks!"

I guess everyone dealt with that moment in his own private way. I was numb and quiet, choking back an avalanche of emotions that came crashing through my mind as I stared out the window at the ribbon of

China Beach receding in the distance. The flashbacks and memories of close calls and painful ordeals kept blinking on and off in my mind like a strobe light. All of a sudden, tears started rolling down my cheeks. The guy next to me asked me if I was all right and I just mumbled, "I don't know."

"Hey, I hear you, man," was his understanding reply.

I guess the months of pent-up emotions — the anger, the hurt, the disillusionment — had come rushing to the surface at that moment of release. With it had come an awareness that I had really survived and was actually going home. I had been wound tighter than a steel cable for so long the tension finally snapped and I was coming apart inside. I was going home in one piece, but I was a casualty nonetheless.

Those of us who endured the long night of Nam and lingered in its shadow know above all how painful the ordeal, how lasting the scars. Some men come home from war with physical wounds. Others are afflicted with more subtle scars.

Some came home from Vietnam in reusable aluminum caskets, some on medevac flights without arms or legs or eyes, while untold thousands returned in the comfort of a commercial airliner like I did. Outwardly everything appeared normal, but inwardly we were psychologically shattered — whole in body, but broken in mind and spirit, a quiet company of men and women wounded within.

Less than twenty-four hours after taking off from Da Nang I arrived at LAX exhausted and wrung out. The awareness that I had made it home still hadn't sunk in. It seemed so bizarre that only the day before

I had been in Vietnam and now I was standing in the Greyhound bus station waiting for a bus to take me home to Tuscaloosa. It all seemed so strange, like some fractured dream. My surroundings had suddenly changed, but I hadn't. They had taken me out of the war, but the war hadn't been taken out of me.

Standing there in a daze, holding my sea bag over my shoulder, I realized that I wasn't ready to go home and face the pain I had left behind. It was too much, too soon. I just wasn't ready to cope with the pressure. I guess I had reached my limit.

I walked across the crowded terminal and fished for a nickel and dropped it into the pay phone and called my uncle in Birmingham. My Uncle Joe and Aunt Ruth had been good to me when I was a kid and had been a refuge on a few occasions when I was growing up. The phone rang twice. I heard my Uncle Joe's voice answer on the other end of the line. "Hello," he said.

There was a long pause and then he asked again, "Hello, is anyone there?"

I took a deep breath and let it out, "Uncle Joe, it's me, Mac." I got choked up and my voice faltered, "I...I'm back. I just got back from Vietnam and I was wondering if I could stay with you for a few days before I go home."

"Mac, Mac! Gosh it's good to hear your voice, son. Sure you can stay with us. Ruth, it's Mac," I could hear him yelling to my aunt. "Where are you now?" he asked. "We'll be right down to pick you up when you get in."

When I arrived in Birmingham they took me in with a quiet understanding — especially my Uncle Joe, who had fought against the Japanese in the South Pacific and had seen the Marines raising the flag on Mount Suribachi on Iwo Jima. I'm sure he understood better than most that I needed some time. The look in my eyes must have told them volumes. I may not have manifested that thousand-yard stare of shell-shocked soldiers straggling back to the rear, but the haggard look revealed something deeper, something almost haunting. My eyes were windows to a pained and troubled soul.

My uncle and aunt let me have a spare room in the back and tried not to bother me by asking me a lot of stupid questions, like "What was it like?" "How bad was it?" or "How many gooks did you kill?" They brought me food and casually checked on me every so often to see if I needed anything, but they mostly just gave me what I needed — space.

I was so withdrawn and felt so confused. I was back in the world, back in the good old "US of A," but I didn't know if I belonged anymore. I felt so betrayed by my country and so out of place. I was tortured with bitterness for having fought a thankless war for a contemptuous and ungrateful nation. I didn't even want to see anyone or let anyone know I had been in Vietnam. It was like I was dislocated — like I had been displaced. I didn't know where I belonged or where to go from here. Nothing seemed to make any sense. I'd made it back alive, but I couldn't put the past behind me, especially at night. I couldn't sleep on a soft bed with clean sheets, so I slept in the bathtub — secretly fearing that I might need the protection. Night was always the worst. I'd sit in that back bedroom with the lights off, staring through the glass panes trying to numb out and forget. Eventually, I would crawl off to the bathtub then slump into a fitful sleep.

The conditioning and sustained pressures of Vietnam had destroyed any semblance of normalcy. Even the simplest movements or sounds could trigger instant responses — a walk across a lawn, the backfire of a passing car, the unexpected tap on the shoulder, the sound of a helicopter passing harmlessly overhead, or being suddenly awakened from sleep.

After a week Uncle Joe called my mom. They knew she would want to know that I was back. My mom had kept up on the news and had worried herself sick many a night after hearing that the Da Nang base had gotten hit with rockets or some big battle had taken place. It was harder in some ways, I think, for those loved ones who were left behind with their uncertainties and fears. Like my girlfriend, my mom had faithfully written, even though I seldom did. When I did I just penned small talk, like how beautiful the sunsets could be, or how things were pretty quiet — never anything about how miserable or dangerous it really was.

After about ten days I said goodbye to my uncle and aunt and caught the bus for Tuscaloosa and home. When I stepped off the bus I gave my mom a hug and said it was good to be home, but I could see by the concerned look on her face that she knew something had changed inside of me. I guess I had shut out the feelings, and had told myself so many times that "it don't mean nothin'" when something bad had happened, that I had just dried up like an old piece of cardboard. I'd closed off the feelings and shut out everyone for so long that I just didn't have anything left to give. Somewhere along the line I died inside and became a cold shell of a man who no longer knew how to love or live.

After a couple of days I decided to go see my girlfriend. I hadn't written in a couple of months. I could tell by the last few letters I had received in Nam that she was agonizing over my silence. I felt that at least I owed her a visit. We had been so close in high school, and had even talked of marriage and children. She and her folks had been the only wholesome and normal things I had known during high school. Her father had taken an interest in me and treated me well, even though he knew I was from the rough side of the tracks, maybe because he saw that I treated their daughter well. I headed over to her house knowing that I owed it to her mom and dad as well.

My girlfriend's parents were overjoyed to see me. When I asked if she was home they told me she was working as a bank teller downtown and would be getting off work soon. Her dad came up with an idea for me to wear his hat and coat and take his car to pick her up when she got off work. I felt stupid but went along with the idea for their sake.

When she came out of the bank and walked up to the car I rolled down the window. When she recognized me she let out a scream of delight. She was so glad to see me that she couldn't stop hugging and kissing me, saying, "Oh, Mac, you're home. I've missed you so much. I've dreamed of this moment for so long that it seems like forever." I halfheartedly hugged her back, but I felt nothing. It felt like I was dead inside. I tried to act the same as before, but a distance had grown between us that only I was aware of. I had grown worlds apart, half a world away. She wanted to be close to me, but I had shut off the feelings for everything and everyone for so long that I just couldn't find it within myself to return the warmth and love she had so faithfully carried for me.

It didn't take long for her to realize something was very wrong. One day we were sitting in her father's car. She was real quiet. Her hands were folded on her lap. She had this sad puppy-dog look on her face. I remember her speaking softly and saying, "Mac, I don't know what's wrong, but I know there's something wrong." She turned and looked at me with her big eyes welling with tears. "Don't you love me anymore?" she pleaded.

"Yea...sure," I said in an unconvincing voice, but she knew. My words had no heart or soul left in them. "What about the wedding?" she asked. I think she knew deep down inside that there wasn't going to be any wedding.

There was no way around it. I had to tell her there wasn't going to be any wedding. I knew it was ripping her apart, but I had to do it because I didn't want to hurt her more in the long run. She didn't know about all the loose women I had been with and the venereal disease I had gotten in Nam from cheap prostitutes. She had been a good girl and pure at heart, and I just didn't want to violate her. She deserved better than that.

A week later my leave was up, and I returned to San Diego to finish out my enlistment.

The Cave

•••

I returned to San Diego dreading six more months of stateside duty with all of its petty "spit and polish" harassment. I was only going back to do my time and count off the days until I could get out of the service. Those two weeks of leave had done little to unravel the tangled knot of confusion and unrest in my heart. I returned to duty, not knowing if I would ever be the same again or how to escape the turmoil I felt.

When I got back I started hanging out at a local bar called "The Cave," in Oceanside. It was a popular hangout for bikers. I would head over to the bar after duty and try to unwind by drinking. At first I kept to myself and sat in a dark corner of the bar checking things out. No one hassled me because I kept to myself. They probably figured I was just a weekend "Roody-poot." I soon noticed that the bikers who frequented the place shared a closeness and camaraderie — much like some of the guys in Nam had shared. I would soon discover that they were a brotherhood who had dropped out of the normal cadence of society. The mainstream considered them to be lowlife, but the "Cave men" could have cared less what society thought. As far as the biker brotherhood was concerned, if you weren't one of them you weren't worth having anything to do with. They did their own thing and stuck together with a special kinship and sense of belonging that I had only briefly encountered in my past.

It was there, sitting by myself in that dimly lit corner one night, that I remembered that sense of belonging I felt as a little boy — the only times I had ever really felt close to my dad — when I had my arms wrapped around my dad's waist cruising together down the back roads of Texas on his old Indian motorcycle. I remembered hugging my dad and how free I felt with the rumble of that motorcycle between our legs, with the wind blowing through our hair as we raced down an open stretch of road. I think the thrill of rushing down a ribbon of asphalt had been in my blood for a long time. My dad had planted that seed in me a long time before. It just took being around those bikers and seeing their closeness to bring it all back. It was the thing I had missed most and the escape I was secretly longing for to soothe the confusion and hurt I was carrying deep in my heart.

I had saved up some money during my tour in Vietnam and decided to buy a motorcycle that fit my personality. It would be my ticket out of my personal hell. I thought about getting a vintage Indian like my dad had owned, but the few I found for sale cost too much. I finally found a chopped Harley shovelhead that fit me like a glove. The gas tank was painted a metallic, candy-apple red, and the bike was tricked out with chrome plating. I remember straddling the chopper, pushing it upright. Man, when I kicked it over, that engine came to life with a roar of power that sent a jolt through me. I knew right then that it had my name written all over it.

It's hard to describe the rush of excitement and surge of adrenaline that comes over you when you accelerate onto a freeway, cutting traffic at 115 miles per hour, passing cars like they were standing still with the divider lines shooting by you like Morse code. It was like a mind-altering drug, a roller-coaster rush, another world that helped ease the pain and help me forget.

I got myself a little apartment down by the beach a couple of blocks from The Cave. A lot of Cave men lived in that area. I started hanging out at The Cave, getting to know some of the bikers that were regulars. Many were Nam vets I felt like I could talk to. It was their hangout, and a place with lots of action — fistfights, stabbings, drug dealing, prostitution, and gambling. It was a fitting name for a den of iniquity where a lot of stuff went down.

Some of the guys were vets like me, so we immediately connected. We'd sit around and get drunk and talk about it between ourselves. We never talked about it with others, because it was "our thing." We knew that outsiders either didn't care or didn't understand. The closeness you felt when you found a fellow brother-in-arms who had been through the same hell in the same places as you was really overwhelming. There was a real bond between us, a quiet understanding that went beyond words, an almost sacred sense of brotherhood that had been forged in the crucible of combat.

We were a family who stuck together through thick and thin — "One for all, all for one." Mess with one, you messed with all. Even when a fight broke out among us, the bottom line was like a domestic disturbance: God help the outsider who tried to interfere.

One day I was buying some parts for my Harley and this big dude walked out of the back of the shop right past me. I'd never seen any biker quite like him. He was wearing tinted aviator glasses, steel-shanked boots with chains draped around them, a black leather jacket cut off at the shoulders, black leather chaps, a big brass buckle with an eagle and swastika embossed upon it, and some serious tattooed sleeves down to his wrists. He had a look of confident defiance and controlled meanness that told everyone to "get out of my way or I'll rip your heart out and feed it to you." He walked past me with his head up and his shoulders squared. Everyone in the shop just stood aside. I'd never seen anything like it — like he was an apparition or something, like he was bigger than life. He went outside and fired up his chopper. It was chopped to the max with no front fender and was completely black.

Everyone in the store was just staring out the window at the guy like they were in a trance. I walked out into the parking lot as he was cranking over his old panhead and pulling away in a throaty roar. I wanted to talk to him, but it was too late. There were a couple of greasy wrenches squatting down in the parking lot working on a bike. I walked over and asked them, "Hey, who is that guy?"

"Man, don't you know nothin'?" they said, spitting out the words like I was a complete bonehead.

"Man, I'm askin' you a simple question," I said in a menacing voice. I wasn't yet a full-fledged biker, but I'd gotten to a place where I had a very short fuse and didn't take lip from anybody. "I asked you who he was."

One of the grease monkeys looked up and said in a softer tone of voice, "Man, that's a Hell's Angel. He's one of the main guys. You don't want to mess with them if you know what's good for you."

From that moment on I knew that I wanted to be just like that guy. He had the look I wanted. In short order the Harley Davidson spirit took hold. I was going through a real transformation. It was a consciousness, a mindset, a feeling of freedom, an attitude of complete defiance. It was a "don't mess with me, I'm doing my own radical thing" mentality. I started talking different, walking different, dressing different, and thinking different.

Over the ensuing weeks I started getting to know some of the Cave men who hung out at The Cave and the repair shop where they bought parts and got their bikes worked on. They were a closeknit family. They drew a tight circle around themselves which didn't admit newcomers easily, but they got to know me and gradually I was accepted. The feeling of being accepted was unbelievable. It was like the homecoming I never got when I came back from Vietnam and, back then, it was the greatest thing that had happened to me. They had seen me handle myself well in a bar fight at The Cave using my karate skills when I put away a couple of macho truckers. They also knew I was a Vietnam vet who'd just gotten back. It helped, too, that I started stealing a lot of military equipment and weapons from the base and drugs from the dispensary and funneling them through the Cave men. Gradually they began to warm up to me. They started inviting me to ride along with them on their weekend runs out to McCain's Valley or the Devil's Punch Bowl to party down.

I can't describe the sense of togetherness they shared and the thrill of cranking all those choppers up before a run. What a sound! The exhilaration of a bunch of idling Harleys and a pack of bikers rackin' our pipes before we pulled out with our mamas wrapped around us and a weekend of partying ahead was almost intoxicating! Those weekends were one long drunken blowout, getting so stoned out of our gourds we couldn't see straight — wild weekends around bonfires seeing who could drink the most and fight the longest until he passed out.

During the week I played it straight, but when my weekend pass started I was out there! I'd throw off my uniform, put on my boots and leathers, and be out of there like the Road Runner. For six months I played by the Navy's Mickey-Mouse rules during the week and was back in the fast lane when the weekends came.

The day I finally got my discharge from the Navy I walked out the front gate and unchained my Harley from a nearby tree. My first act of defiance was to tear off my uniform and throw it into the dirt. I put on my blue jeans, biker boots, and leather jacket and started jumping up and down on my uniform, cursing the Navy and grinding my clothes into the dirt. I was so angry and bitter about the government for how it had treated us. I was bitter about the waste and the hurt it had inflicted on so many of us who had served in good faith. Even the ones who had come home to rot in some forsaken VA hospital were often treated with contempt, like they were some kind of parasite or disease.

Those last six months in the service had changed me. They had added to the bitterness and anger seething inside of me. They had driven me into the waiting arms of a brotherhood who understood and a lifestyle that offered me a way to vent the hatred I felt.

The biker brotherhood was a perfect haven for a lot of vets like me who came home disillusioned and embittered — for men who came home to protests and profanity rather than pride and patriotism. For those vets who gave so much and came home to so little, the acceptance and brotherhood of the outlaw gangs was a much-needed home. Not only were the outlaw gangs extremely patriotic and fought anybody who put down America or condemned those who fought for her, they really stood shoulder to shoulder with the Vietnam vets. About 90 percent of outlaw bikers are veterans. For a lot of disgruntled and disillusioned vets who didn't come home to waving flags, marching bands, yellow ribbons, or thanks for a job well done, the biker brotherhood offered a sanctuary and welcome home that was missing. We found a measure of satisfaction and a sense of revenge in the biker philosophy, which said to society, "If this is what you are going to do to me, then this is what I am going to do to you!" The biker brotherhood was a way for angry young men to ventilate the rage of disgust they held against those who had turned their backs on them. It was a renegade lifestyle that rejected the society that rejected them.

I unlocked the chain from my Harley that discharge day, fired it up, and began my descent into the biker underground. I headed out that day into the sunset, bound and determined to join its ranks.

CHAPTER 7

Mac the Maniac

• • •

Once I'd discarded the remains of my life in the military I plunged headlong into the biker lifestyle. I wasn't a "weekend wannabe" any longer. Whitewalls were out. Hair was in. I let it grow and stopped shaving. By the speed of the transformation I was undergoing, you would have thought I was going through the changes of a werewolf at midnight.

The memories of Vietnam were still with me, but they had lost some of their intensity in the camaraderie of my biker buddies and the fast life I was now living. But the adrenaline rush I was racing on was only a temporary distraction from the pain I carried inside. The drugs and booze softened the sharp edges that pricked at my heart. The defiance of the club helped unleash the flood of pent-up anger that was raging inside of me, but it couldn't stem the tide. The guys I rode with didn't care what anyone thought, but at least we didn't care together.

A steady flow of drugs and booze required a constant source. The men I was riding with had established a network of contacts for drug buys through connections south of the border. Since Tijuana was one of my former hangouts while in the Navy, I started scoring drugs there and running them up the coast from Mexico for distribution and sales. It was a way for us to make money quick and keep ourselves supplied and stoned at the same time. I was buying bricks of pot and bags of speed we called "White Cross."

In no time I was taking large quantities and getting pretty strung out. The drugs only accelerated the pace of the lifestyle I was living. If I wasn't zipping down the interstate on my chopper I was flying inside from the rush of crank. But, like all mind-altering drugs, the euphoria and chemical high soon begin to turn on you and show you their dark side. I started getting really spaced out, unpredictable, and paranoid.

We were out for an "afternoon putt" with some of our old ladies when we pulled into a truck stop to get something to eat. We were sitting by the window when the waitress came up to our booth — you know, one of those "Thelma Jean" types with ratted, red hair and sequined glasses who looked like she had just been voted "Queen of the Truck Stop." She was chewing a wad of gum and holding her receipt book, waiting to take our order.

"Whatd'ya have?" she said.

"I'll have a burger and fries and some coffee," I responded. But she just stood there smacking her gum looking down at me like I was a Martian or something.

I figured she was a little dense, so I told her again, "Give me a burger, fries, and coffee."

But she just stood there looking at me and smacking her gum like I was speaking Swahili.

"Listen, I ain't gonna tell you again," I said. "I want you to bring me a burger, fries, and some coffee!" I said, slamming my fist down on the table.

"Hey, Mac, cool it!" Ratman said as I swept the table clean in a shower of broken glass and utensils.

"Sit down, Mac!" Ratman growled.

I had jumped to my feet and overturned the table. Then I went berserk. People were screaming. My buddies were yelling for me to stop before the cops came. I was hurling chairs at the mirrors behind the counter and throwing over tables with plates of food on them. I was completely flipped out.

The brothers grabbed me, shouting in my ear, "Let's get outta here, man. The cops are gonna come. You're causin' too much of a scene. We're holding too much stuff and the cops are gonna bust us good if they get here."

They finally pulled me out of the diner. We jumped on our bikes, cranked them up, and roared off down the road.

When we finally got to where we were going they really came down on me.

"Man, when we're out on the streets we've got to be the most law abidin' people 'cause we don't want any extra heat comin' down on us," they said.

That night we were sitting around a crackling bonfire passing joints and cans of beer when Ratman said, "Man, what got into you? You lost it or something? You can't be actin' like that. You're going to get us all busted. You got to show some more cool."

"But I ordered three times and the old bag didn't bring me my order," I protested.

"What are ya talkin' about. You crazy or somethin'?" Ratman said "You didn't say anything. You never said a word. We all thought you were playing some kind of mind game or somethin' because you just sat there with this stone-cold expression on your face looking at that waitress when she asked you for your order."

"Man, I ordered three times!" I yelled.

"We're tellin' you like it is, Mac. You never opened your mouth."

I started swearing. "I know I did!"

"Calm down, Mac. Chill out, man. Hey, it's okay. We've all been there."

"Just a bad trip." One of the mamas patted me on the back.

"Man, Mac, you must've been wired for sound, dude, 'cause you were totally out there this time," another commented.

"I guess I was pretty wasted," I said.

"Yeah, big guy, a real space cadet," someone responded.

"You should have seen yourself, man. You were a real maniac today!" another added. "Like we said, man, you got to be a real law abidin' dude out there so the cops won't pull you over."

"Hey, that's it! 'Mac, the maniac,'" Ratman said as the circle busted up laughing.

I had been doing so much speed my mind was fried. It was racing at light speed. I guess I had been so wiped out that I was hallucinating in the diner and actually thought the gal had been ignoring me.

I was turning into a real speed freak. But that didn't stop me from taking more. I kept popping pills and drinking booze like it was going out of style. In time the highs flattened out. I needed a heavier dose and longer rushes, so I started eating acid and cutting lines of cocaine and snorting them through my nose like a vacuum cleaner. I was getting pretty strung out.

I ate it all, smoked it all, and drank it all, but the one thing I didn't use was the needle. That was one of the few taboos for the biker clubs in the early seventies. You could get higher than a kite or pickle your brain in alcohol, but you didn't shoot dope. Those who did crossed an invisible line of trust as far as the brothers were concerned. A junkie's first loyalty was to the needle, not the brotherhood. Needle freaks just couldn't be trusted and were a real liability. Start hitting up and you were out.

I had one brother everybody liked, named "Little Joe." He was a wiry little guy, as tough as barbed wire. He carried an equalizer stuck in his boot to make up for his size. He never backed away from anybody — as ferocious as a pit bull. The little dude was crazy just like me. Maybe that's why we got along so well. We'd be up in McCain's Valley partying hardy around a roaring bonfire. We'd grip each other's hands and just start squeezing with sick grins on our faces. Our hands were locked in a vise-grip, squeezing the life out of each other. We'd stand there drunker than gutter winos, staring each other in the eyes, playing a mind game with each other. Then we'd take turns center punching each other in the chest with our free hand, punching each other to see who would be the first to let go.

When we'd get into one of those contests everyone would drop what they were doing and gather around. It was a real event. Any other time guys could be slapping the daylights out of their old ladies or doing all kinds of twisted things and the party would just keep rolling on, but when Little Joe and I squared off like two mountain goats everything would stop.

That little guy and I were real tight, but even so, when he started mainlining heroin, the guys decided he had to leave.

I was sinking deeper and deeper into a cesspool of sin and perversity, but I didn't care. I was a runaway train completely out of control. I couldn't have put on the brakes if I'd wanted to. Deep down inside I was still poisoned by an abscess of guilt, bitterness, and hate, which infected my soul. The pain was driving me further down a path of self-destruction.

I'd left the weekend warrior thing far behind. I was completely into the lifestyle. I was scoring drugs on regular runs to supply the club and reveling in the fleshpots of Tijuana on my cross-border drug excursions. I began to go down there to pick up thirteen- and fourteen-year-old prostitutes. You could buy or see any perversity in Tijuana with the right color of money. These little Mexican pimps would line the streets and call out their deals like carnival barkers.

"Hey, gringo, you want to buy virgin? Hey, amigo, you want to be with my mother? Come with me, gringo; my sister is ready for you," they would shout out their propositions from the sidewalks and alley ways.

In little more than a year I had degenerated into one very sick puppy. My hair was down to my shoulders and I had sprouted an enormous bushy beard that made me look like some deranged Saint Nick. It was so unkept and filthy that "little critters" actually lived in it. On more than one occasion I woke up out in the desert or under a car after sleeping off a drunk and found bugs crawling around my beard looking for scraps of food. I was really into grossing people out. I thrived on their reaction. I wasn't only one ugly dude, I smelled like I had crawled out of some sewer. I never bathed, never shaved, and never washed my clothes.

However, I had begun to climb up the pecking order and establish my rank among my biker brotherhood. I'd proven myself in one fight after another and had shown them how brutal I could be in a fight with my karate skills and bulldog tenacity. I seldom lost and, even when I did, I never backed down.

I'd quickly earned a reputation for being a wild man through my willingness to do the craziest things. I wasn't afraid of anything. I never turned down the most insane dare. The brothers would joke around with me and say, "Hey, big Mac, here's another pack of razor blades for you to eat. Mac, show them what you can do, man. It'll blow your mind. He's an animal. Watch him. The guy will eat anything, and if you get in his way he'll chew your arms and legs off and eat them too. 'Mac, the maniac,' we call him."

I had never had much support from my parents growing up. They never showed any interest in my school work or came to any of my football games, even though I was a star player on the team and made "All State" and received honorable mention in the newspapers. Maybe they were just too overwhelmed with their own conflicts to care. But the attention from my biker brothers was something I thrived on and craved.

On one of our weekend runs up to McCain's Valley we were sitting around the bonfire passing joints and bottles of tequila, spacing out on the popping sparks, when this monster biker rumbles up on an old hog. The guy had to be six-foot-six and weigh a good 350 plus.

He swung an enormous shank over his chopper seat and lumbered over to the bonfire like a big gorilla. The way he carried himself you would have thought he was about to drop to all fours and start walking on his knuckles. He was the fattest, ugliest dude I had ever seen. He thudded into the dirt without a word. He didn't do anything at first until he started fondling my old lady. When she told him to get his fat fingers off of her I stood up and told him we were going to rumble.

Well, he rose up, glared at me for a moment, then charged me like a rogue elephant. As soon as he lunged I charged back. We hit each other in a head-on collision. It looked like two sumo wrestlers crashing into each other. It was all I could do to stay on my feet. Arms and fists were flying. I was landing some good blows, but hitting his head was like hitting concrete. I was slugging away, but my blows were having about as much effect as throwing marshmallows at a stone wall. I felt like I was fighting Godzilla. The guy was taking everything I had and still coming at me. He threw one powerful roundhouse that snapped my head back, then followed through by driving his other fist right into my mouth, smashing my lips and splattering blood and teeth all over the place. Blood was spurting everywhere. I knew that I couldn't hold on much longer.

All I remember was a bunch of my buddies pulling us off of each other and yelling that we had to get out of there because the cops were coming. A sheriff's car had come up the dirt road to check out the bonfire. The sheriff saw the fight and called for backup. You could hear sirens in the distance. Everyone was running helter-skelter trying to get out of there. Women were screaming and guys were cranking up their choppers. Several squad cars pulled up with their lights flashing and deputies started piling out and wading into the chaos, macing people and swinging night sticks as bikes and pickups roared off across the valley, fishtailing and churning up clouds of dirt.

I don't remember much after King Kong knocked my front teeth out except being carried to a car and thrown in the trunk. I woke up the next morning looking like someone had worked me over with a baseball bat. My face was black and blue and engorged with blood.

I remember one of the guys saying, "Mac, I don't know how you stayed with that guy as long a you did!"

"I guess he really messed me up," I said through lips that looked like they'd gone through a meat grinder.

"Yeah, but you should have seen him. He wasn't going to win any beauty contests either, big guy. Man, only 'Mac the maniac' could have taken that moose on," he noted.

"Well, at least I learned one thing last night," I said. "No matter how big and bad you think you are, there is always gonna be someone bigger and badder than you!"

I didn't have much in the looks department before that fight, but I looked even meaner and crazier afterward. With my front teeth knocked out all I had left was a cavernous opening with my two eye teeth hanging down like fangs on a vampire. I was one pretty scary sight to behold.

Alabama Bound

• • •

Living the fast life with my newfound family hadn't given me much occasion to think about anyone back home. I had done my best to distance myself from everything I had left behind. No one knew where my dad had run off to, and all that was left was a broken mom who spent her time smoking cigarettes and drinking cheap vodka in an attempt to drown a lifetime of sorrows. Still, my mom loved me and worried about me. She wrote, but I didn't write back. She'd call and ask why I wasn't coming home and I'd tell her I was entering college and was pretty busy. I didn't tell her what I had fallen into. It would only have broken a heart already fractured from a lifetime of hurt.

But in her heart she knew something was wrong and begged me to come home. Like me, she harbored a world of guilt — feeling that she had failed as a mother even though she had done her best. Like all loving mothers, she loved me unconditionally, no matter what I was doing, and longed to have me home — free of whatever I was into. Finally her pleading struck a cord. I decided to drop out of the brotherhood for a while and go home. I could sense that my mother was slowly destroying herself, and I didn't want that to happen. I guess we were each casualties of our pasts. Each of us was dealing with our wounds in our own way. She suffered in silence with her pint of vodka, while I suffered through a life of wanton abandon. Deep down inside I knew that I had reached a place of reckless insanity that was destroying me too. I guess I sensed that going home was a way out — a way to get my head back together.

I didn't want to tell my brothers that I was divorcing the family, because I loved them, too, so I told them I was going back to Alabama to check out the possibilities of setting up a drug network and to try to recruit some new brothers. I told them I would be back in a few months. I asked them to keep my chopper and take care of it while I was gone. It was the only thing I owned that meant anything. The guys escorted me in formation to the bus depot and gave me quite a send-off. It just wouldn't be the same without "Mac, the maniac" around.

As the Greyhound pulled out of the terminal I waved goodbye to my brothers and settled into my seat for the long ride across the Southwest. I must have been a disgusting sight in my biker garb with my patches and chains. I can't imagine what those poor passengers endured for two thousand miles. I looked appalling, with my greasy crop of hair, enormous beard, and toothy fangs. I reeked of old sweat and road filth. It didn't bother me, because I'd grown used to it. But as far as those hapless passengers were concerned I must have looked and smelled like a piece of toxic waste. My seat in the back of the bus quickly became a dead zone to everyone around me.

That was fine with me. I'd grown pretty paranoid and territorial. My conditioning in Nam had bred a wariness that always made me want to know where everyone was and what was going on around me. I didn't like strangers getting close. To make sure, I put out vibes to let everyone know that they had better back off or else. It was okay for the brothers to be close, even to greet each other with a "center punch," but that was because we trusted each other and knew that we would stand by each other's side no matter who the foe or what the odds.

Our biker lifestyle had nurtured a distrust and suspicion of anyone who wasn't one of us, so sitting on that bus was a struggle for all on board. If you were a "citizen" we wouldn't have anything to do with you. If you didn't ride a Harley you weren't a real biker to us. No real biker rode one of those foreign-made vacuum cleaners or "rice burners," — none of that Jap scrap, "trumpets," or "beezers." Only wannabees and wimps rode those. It had to be a Harley Davidson. It had to be American steel.

Being an outlaw biker attracted the attention of the cops. Everywhere we rode they were sure to follow. The "man" was always hassling us and pulling us over to cite us or try to bust us for carrying drugs or weapons. Because the police were always shadowing us we lived in a perpetual state of paranoia. It was that frame of mind I carried onto the bus for that long trip home.

The escort we picked up when we crossed the Louisiana border hadn't helped. Somewhere along the line, at one of our rest stops, the driver or one of the passengers must have alerted the police and informed them that there was a dangerous-looking character on board. Different police agencies took turns tailing the bus, making sure nothing happened. By the time we rolled into Tuscaloosa we had three state troopers shadowing us. I'd called ahead and told my mother to pick me up at the Greyhound station, but I didn't tell her the cops were following right behind.

When the bus pulled into the terminal the passengers hurriedly piled out. Maybe they were extra glad the trip was over — relieved that they wouldn't have to be riding with me any longer. I was the last one off. When I walked into the lobby I scanned the crowd, trying to see if mom was waiting. That's when I caught her face anxiously looking around. She didn't even recognize me, which wasn't hard to understand when you considered the mangy-looking creature who had just stepped off the bus. I looked like some prehistoric caveman with dark shades, Dracula-looking fangs, and a body stink that could peel paint off a wall. I guess she had been waiting for the crowd of passengers to get off the bus and had a disappointed look on her face when I stepped off last. Everyone had disembarked and she hadn't seen me. She walked right past me, then glanced back one more time and finally looked me in the eyes for the first time. That's when it registered. I'd taken off my sunglasses and was just standing there with my arms folded across my chest.

"Mac? Mac Gober?" she asked hesitantly.

"Yeah, Mom, it's me all right," I grinned a stupid grin with my pointed fangs showing. "What's the matter, Mom, don't you recognize me?" I said.

I grabbed her in a big bear hug and lifted her off her feet. "You still my favorite girl, Mom?" I asked playfully.

"Put me down! Put me down right this minute, Mac," she demanded as I swung her around the lobby filled with the startled faces of travelers.

"What's gotten into you, Mac? What happened to you?" she said as she looked me up and down.

"Don't I look handsome, Mom?" I tried to make light of the situation.

She was completely caught off guard by the shock of my appearance. She immediately started grilling me with the first degree, asking all kinds of concerned "mother" questions.

I didn't want to confirm her worst fears, so I made up some lies about working out in California, how times were tough, and how I wasn't doing so well in school because I had to work so much. I didn't say anything about the guns, the drug dealing, or the prostitution.

As soon as we got into her car and pulled away from the curb a couple of state troopers pulled up behind us and started following us as we wound our way through the city and headed north on the interstate.

"Mac, why are those police cars following us?" my mom asked as she looked in the rearview mirror and double-checked her speedometer.

"Aw, don't worry, Mom; I'm clean," I told her.

She turned and looked at me like I must have lost my mind, too, because I was the raunchiest, filthiest, stinkiest human being she'd ever seen.

"Clean! Son, you're filthy. Is that what you call clean?" she asked incredulously.

I could tell she didn't know what I meant, so I said, "I'm clean, Mom. I'm not holding anything. I don't have any drugs on me, Mom. They can't bust me for anything." I chuckled. She didn't know any street slang, so she had no idea what I was talking about.

"It's okay, Mom, just keep drivin'. They ain't gonna do anything."

"But why are they following us?" my mother asked with fear in her voice.

"Ah, they probably think I'm somebody else," I reassured her.

It wasn't long before I found out where some of the local bikers hung out. They weren't as organized or hard core as my brothers back on the West Coast, but they were willing wannabee candidates. Many of them had heard of me. I had taken on a celebrity status during my absence. I would drop by to rap with them and score the drugs I needed by telling them biker war stories, but I wanted to lay low and keep the heat from breathing down my neck. I didn't want my mom freaking out by having the cops sniffing around.

I got a job that fit my skills and experience — a bouncer at one of the popular road houses outside of Tuscaloosa. It was a favorite hang-out for road types and good old southern rednecks. It was a pretty rowdy place, but when anyone stepped out of line I'd bust his head and throw him out of the bar. I had my piece tucked into my blue jeans for extra backup. I'd just lean up against the wall with a sinister, intimidating look on my face, surveying the bar crowd with my dark sunglasses, biker boots, and chains, and my pistol stuck in my waistline. Needless to say, one look at me from a rowdy drunk was usually enough to cool things down. The crowd who hung out there soon learned that you didn't mess with Mac.

One evening this big dude walked into the bar like he was The Terminator. He was throwing himself around like he was the toughest man alive, bragging about how bad he was. He was cussing and challenging patrons to try and take him on. I got a practiced nod from the bartender.

I slipped up behind him without his seeing my approach, pulled out my snub-nosed .38, grabbed a big lock of his hair, then jerked his head back and stuck the tip of my revolver up his nose.

"Think you're pretty bad?" I whispered in his ear. I had the hammer cocked back and my finger on the trigger.

"How bad do you really think you are? You really want to impress all these people?" I hissed as I twisted his head sideways to see the crowd who had gathered around. His eyes were bugging out and he had a terrified expression on his face.

"Don't shoot me!" he pleaded.

"How 'bout you and me steppin' outside and we'll see how bad you really are. You been itching for a fight, so here I am, tough guy," I said.

"Please don't pull the trigger, man. I've heard about you. Listen," he said, "I'm really sorry. I didn't mean nothin'."

"C'mon, punk, you and me are going outside and see what kinda man you can be," I said as I gripped his hair and pushed him forward with my gun still stuck in his nose. "If you've heard of me, you haven't heard half the story," I taunted him.

"Please don't kill me," he begged.

I'd rammed that snub-nosed barrel far enough into his nose that a trickle of blood was running down his lips.

"You don't want to sneeze, 'cause this here gun has a hair trigger and it might just go off. We wouldn't want that, would we?" I said in a sadistic tone.

I pushed him through the front door and propelled him out into the parking lot. A large crowd followed us out. They were rooting me on like I was a gladiator getting ready to finish off my opponent.

"Which one of these cars is yours?" I threatened.

"That one over there," he nodded slightly. "The white Dodge."

I pushed him up against the car with my revolver trained on him and said, "Roll down the window."

"What...what are you going to do?" he asked with a panicked strain in his voice as he cranked down the driver's side window.

"Shut up and stick your arm through the window." "Jesse," I said to one of the guys who worked at the club, "roll up the window."

Jesse flashed me a sadistic grin and started cranking up the car window.

"Aeah...Aeeah," the guy was screaming as the window edge started crushing his arm.

I kicked the door shut with him caught in it, slamming him up against the car. "Okay, big boy, we're going to entertain the crowd now," I said. "How good can you dance?" I asked as I squeezed off several measured rounds at his feet.

The guy was screaming and crying, begging me to let him go. "Please don't kill me. Please don't kill me!" He was sobbing like a little boy.

"Hey, would Big Mac do that?" I said, mockingly. "I just wanted to show all these good people how tough you really are."

"Take his arm out, Jesse," I instructed. "Now, big man, everything between you and me is even," I said as I handed the pistol to Jesse and stepped back. "It's just you and me now. You ready to impress all these people?" I asked.

"No. I'm sorry. I was drinking too much and I'm really sorry," he begged.

"Then apologize to all these nice people," I ordered. "Get down on your hands and knees and say you're sorry," I said in a controlled voice. He did. It was pathetic. I had completely broken him.

Man, I was an instant hero. Chicks were coming up to me and telling me how great I was. Guys were slapping me on the back saying, "Way to go, Mac. Outta sight, Mac. You sure showed him, Mac." As a result, my reputation as the meanest bouncer in the county began to grow.

Working as a bouncer in a bar gave me all the booze I wanted. Consequently, I stayed messed up most of the time. What little control I had gained since returning home was starting to slip away. One night I broke up a scuffle and got a little too carried away. The girlfriend of one of the guys called the cops when she saw me beating her boyfriend senseless on the dance floor. When the cops heard my name mentioned they knew it wasn't going to be a routine call. The police had already heard my name circulated on the streets and weren't going to take any chances. They'd already given the management and me warnings that they weren't going to stand by and let me beat up people at will and were just looking for the opportunity to come down on me. When they pulled up that night in front of that honky-tonk with their sirens wailing I stormed out to meet them in a drunken rage. I vaguely remember the shouts and cracking sound of the clubs as they pummeled me with blows and wrestled me to the ground. I can still remember the fluorescent glow of the bar's neon and the flashing lights from the squad cars as the cops struggled to force me into a straitjacket they'd brought along just for me. It took a whole detachment of police to subdue me and take me in that night. They gave me an armload of Thorazine to sedate me. I was thrashing and kicking and spitting, trying to bite them as they fought to restrain me. I was calling them every filthy thing I could think of. I can remember one startled cop telling his partner as they carried me to the car, "God, Darrell, he's an animal! I've never seen anything like it!"

Mac Gober, age 5, with his dad on a 1947 Indian motorcycle

Mac with his mother at Canaan Land. Dr. Jerry Savelle in background

Mac at age 16

With a friend on patrol near the Da Nang River

Back from a Saturday afternoon dive
Between four of us we caught 32 lobsters

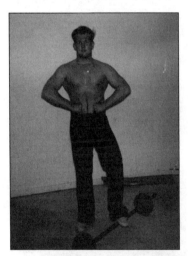

Staying in shape for boxing and getting ready to go to Vietnam

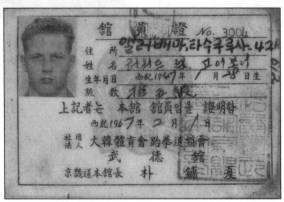

Mac's karate license

Just out of the hospital in Vietnam, with Len Park

BELOW:

Mac giving a karate demonstration in Vietnam

RIGHT

With karate instructor Yong Koo John

Just returned from a bike rally at Sturgis, South Dakota

Mac leading a "trip-wire" vet to the Lord

Mac (left) *with close friend and riding partner Bear Pegram* (center) *and Doug Stadnyk, president of the Tribe of Judah, Saskatchewan chapter*

Close friend Ben Priest, International Boss of the Tribe of Judah

Talking with Kenneth Copeland at an Eagle Mountain bike rally

Jeff Givens, longtime missionary to Haiti, now president of the Mobile, Alabama, chapter of the Tribe of Judah

The author is a keynote speaker at the annual 700 Club's National Vietnam Conference, shown here with Beau Habitnek, who gave his life to the Lord at the conference

Mac Gober, president and founder of Canaan Land Bible Training Center, speaking to students

Mac and Sandra Gober

Rachel Gober

Caleb Gober

Mac, Sandra and their family

Joshua Gober

Poor Old Dirt Farmer

• • •

As my reputation grew, so did the knowledge of my drug dealing. The police were on to me, but they couldn't get enough evidence to put me away. I was making a lot of contacts through the steady traffic at the road house and my links with the local bikers. As a result, the supply and demand began to grow, and with it the need to score new sources.

I decided to head up to my granddad's farm to check out the possibilities of cultivating some marijuana. My granddad and granny lived in a little wooden farmhouse on some property owned by an Episcopalian church near Nauvoo, Alabama. When my granddad was younger he would haul supplies around the county with his team of mules. Now that he was older he and my granny served as caretakers for the Episcopalian youth camp. They supervised the camp in the summer and farmed a small patch of land on the side. My grandparents were one of the few sources of happiness I had known during my childhood summers. For a few joyous weeks during my childhood I would be free from the fighting and drunkenness of my parents — free to play baseball with the kids who came to the camp, free to swim in the creeks, free to explore the trails and hideaways in the backwoods of Alabama. They were times I carried fond memories of. But what I loved the most was the companionship of my granddad and granny.

My granddad was a simple man, but one who had a profound faith in Jesus. He was a man of the field and loved the outdoors. I remember his taking me for long walks in the woods and showing me some of the wonders of nature. We'd walk for hours with his old black dog Drum tagging along with his tail constantly wagging and his nose forever sniffing everything in sight. My granddad would show me all kinds of neat things — like how to take elephant ear grass and make it into a cup to drink the water from the creeks that meandered through the woods. It was a time of discovery and wonder. He really showed me that he loved me and took me wherever he went. I'd work with him in the barn, helping him stack hay with the pitchfork or feed the animals. I remember following behind him and his old mule as they plowed furrows across the warm summer fields. He'd be talking to me and Jesus at the same time, like we were both walking beside him.

My granny would cook me big meals and let me sleep in their old feather bed. I will never forget the smell of her stew cooking on that wood stove or the aroma of hot apple pie filling the house. It was a simple old house with only a potbelly stove to keep it warm but it had a warmth and love that I will never forget.

But what I remember most was their closeness to God. The thing I remember most about my granddad was his love for Jesus. Even on our walks in the woods he would talk to Him like He was right next to us. I never understood it when I was little, but was always taken by how real God seemed to my grandparents. I would play with the church kids who came to the Bible camp for the summer and attend the chapel services with them, but it was all kind of strange to me. My grandparents never forced religion on me or preached at me. Instead, they just loved me in their own simple way.

Their steady influence had its effect while I was at their place, but the constant tension and strife at home inevitably undermined any good that was sown during those brief summer visits.

Looking back to those times of innocence and wonder, I think those brief interludes of love and acceptance planted a tiny seed in my heart. It was sown on the threshold of my adolescence, in the twilight of my youth, when the last vestiges of innocence had begun to fade. It was the one good seed I had done everything in my power to uproot.

By the time I had reached adolescence my trips to see my granddad had ceased, and with them any contact with God. The last time I stepped into a church was when a friend invited me when I was twelve. All I can remember is sitting in the back pew beside my friend, giggling at the formality of it all. He was so embarrassed by my irreverence that he took me outside. He went back in, and I just walked down the road laughing, thinking how lame he was and how stupid it all seemed.

My dad never had anything to do with religion and would often get into heated arguments with my granddad when he'd come to pick me up. I remember asking my father on the car ride home from my grandparents' why he was fighting with granddad. I'd heard them fighting the night before while I was pretending to be asleep in that old feather bed. "Daddy," I asked him from the backseat, "did you ever go to church or think about going?"

He just stared ahead at the road and said in a mocking voice, "Yeah, boy, I went to church, once — before you were born when I came back from the war."

"You did, Daddy?" I asked, a little surprised by his confession.

"That's right, son," he answered. "I had my shirt unbuttoned down to my navel and I was winking at this pretty girl up in the choir when some of the good brethren of the church came down the aisle and asked me to leave. They didn't think I was good enough for their church, so I got up and left. But I went back," he said as he took a long drag off of his cigarette and crushed it out in the ash tray.

"You went back, Daddy," I said, hoping for the best.

"Yeah, that's right. I went back that night after all those good people had left their precious little church," he said with a contemptible tone in his voice. "I went back with a can of gasoline and I burnt that church to the ground. Nobody was going to kick Bill Gober out of that church again. That's the last time I ever stepped inside of a church and that's why your granddad and me are always fighting over religion."

I remember how sad I felt at that moment and I remember looking at my mom. She sat there in silence, looking out the passenger window. That was the first time I heard my dad speak of God or church, and it was the last time. I remember slouching back down in the backseat of our old Ford wondering how my granddad could love God so much and my dad could love Him so little.

That conversation was years before and a lot had changed since then. I had gone to war and run with outlaw motorcycle gangs. My granddad was now bedridden. A tree fell on him while he was clearing some ground on the farm, and he was now paralyzed from the neck down.

I loved my grandparents, but I'd seen a lot and done a lot. My respect and awe had faded over the years. Their love for me never faltered, though. When I returned to visit them they were overjoyed to see me again. I gave them a big hug and acted like I was the same old grandson who had come up to visit them years before. But I was just playing a big game — playing like I was good old Mac, just coming all the way up from Tuscaloosa to visit my dear old grandparents. What I was really interested in was planting a crop of pot and scheming a way to score some more money. I was just using them for my own selfish purposes.

I visited my grandparents regularly after I returned to Tuscaloosa. I would lie to them and tell them I was going for a hike like I did when I was a kid. What I was really doing was finding secret clearings tucked away in the woods. I would plant some choice seeds and tend the seedlings when they started to come up.

I loved my grandparents, but in my heart I thought they had missed out on real life. I remember standing in front of that same old feather bed I had slept on as a kid, staring down at my old granddad just lying there. I'd stand there looking down at his broken body and think to myself, "You poor old dirt farmer. What do you have to show for your life? Where has it gotten you and granny?" I'd stand there in my dirty jeans and bushy beard just shaking my head and feeling pity for that old man.

I remember his looking up at me with love in his eyes and saying, "Son, please don't forget the Lord. Never forget how much He loves you, Mac."

"Don't worry, Granddad, I won't," I would assure him, all the while thinking in the back of my head, "Why should I? Where has it gotten you? Besides, there ain't no way that He is going to love somebody like me. It's too late for that now." I'd see him lying there unable to move, hearing him beg me not to forget the Lord. For a moment I'd want to fall down and tell him all the ugly things I had done. I'd see him there in his condition still loving me. I'd want to get it off my chest by letting all the pain out of me, but I just couldn't. Then the feeling would pass, and I'd say my goodbyes for a few more weeks until I could come back to check on my precious plants.

Flashback

• • •

I walked into the bar early one evening to start my night shift as bouncer. The crowd was thin and the action hadn't picked up yet. Somebody was sweeping the dance floor, and Jack was wiping glasses behind the counter. I was looking around the room, surveying my territory, when I saw a Marine sitting at a table by himself. I couldn't believe my eyes. I did a double take. It was my old buddy Len. He had on his Marine Corps dress greens. He had just gotten back from Vietnam.

"Len!" I shouted across the room. Everyone looked up expecting a fight or something. "Len, man, I don't believe it," I said as I ran across the room.

"Mac!" Len shouted as he stood up.

We embraced each other like long-lost friends. My little Marine buddy had made it back alive.

"Wow, Len, you made it back," I said.

"Yeah, I made it back. There were times I didn't think I would, old buddy, but here I am!"

We had been the best of friends in high school and had enlisted at the recruiter's office on the same day. Our paths crossed briefly in Da Nang when I was sent to the hospital. We had shared our ordeals in the quiet of a dark hospital hallway late one night. We could see by the haggard look on each of our faces that we had changed. While I had done my time along the steamy banks of the Da Nang River, Len had served as a grunt north of Da Nang around Phu Bai and Hue. He spent his thirteen months in hell slopping through the stinking muck of rice paddies and congested tangle of jungle greens. He'd confided in me that lonely night in the hospital that he didn't think he would make it out alive, but here he was in the flesh. Neither of us could really believe it.

Man, we tore that place apart that night. Nobody messed with us. If well-wishers weren't buying us another round of drinks we were taking on anyone who crossed our path. It was a real blowout.

A few days later I returned from a day out at a swimming hole where we partied. I'd been out there with a girl I had been introduced to by a friend. I was sitting at home when the phone rang.

"Hello," I answered the phone.

"Mac, you gotta come now, man. They're all over the place," Len said in a panicked-sounding voice.

"Wait a minute, calm down. What's going down, Lenny? Who's all over the place?" I asked him.

"They're out there, Mac, and they're going to overrun the place. You got to help me, man." Len was really shook up. "I've only got this one shotgun and a few shells left. My old man is in the back, but he's real sick. My little kid brother is here with me, but we're surrounded, Mac. There are three carloads of guys outside, and they're threatening to come in here to kill me. Mac, you've got to come now!"

"Stay cool, man. Your buddy's coming right now, Len. Don't let them overrun your position. Keep your perimeter tight. I'm on my way," I tried to reassure him.

"Man, just hurry!" he pleaded.

"I'll be there as soon as I can," I said as I hung up the phone. I ran for my car.

On my way over I passed another old high school buddy. I waved him over and rolled down my window. "Look, I'm on my way over to Len's. He just called and said a bunch of guys have surrounded his house and are trying to kill him. He needs help. After just getting back from Nam, I'm not about to let some redneck punks kill him now. We've been through too much for me to let that happen. Go try and get some help!"

I was racing down those back roads to Len's house as fast as I could floor it. I figured I would sneak up on the rednecks with the element of surprise in my favor. I slowed the car down and pulled off the road a few hundred yards from Len's house. I cut overland through the woods until I reached the tree line bordering the clearing where Len's old farmhouse lay. It was like being back in the jungle once again. All that jungle juice started pumping through me just like before. I crept up to a wall of bushes near the house to get a closer look. I parted some of the branches, expecting to see a bunch of guys crawling up to the house. But there was no one there. The cars were gone and everything looked quiet. "Oh, no," I thought to myself, "they've already wasted him." I darted from the thicket and ran toward the house. "Don't shoot! It's me, Mac! Len, are you in there?" I yelled, expecting the worst.

Just then the screen door opened, and Len stepped out holding his shotgun with a sheepish grin on his face. "It was a bad one this time, Mac," he said.

"Whatd'ya mean, Len? Did you have a flashback or something?" I asked.

"New, man, it wasn't like that," he replied.

"Man, Len, don't go playing no stupid games with me. I thought you were really in trouble and I raced over here," I said with a tinge of anger in my voice. "You threw me on a complete wild one, man — just like being back in Nam!"

"No, Mac, you got it wrong," Len insisted. "They were here all right. Just a few minutes ago. Man, I wasn't freaking out or anything. It was for real. I'm not lying to you. There were three carloads right here," he said as he gestured with his shotgun.

"Well, what did you do," I asked, "scare them off with the shotgun?"

"No, you ain't gonna believe this, man. It's a real mind blower. They were all out here threatening to come in to get me when my little kid brother walked right out of the house and started laughing. They didn't know what to make of it. Then he said to them, 'You guys are in big trouble now. Y'all just wait. My big brother just called Mac Gober, and he's on his way over. Ha, ha, ha, ha, ha!'

"As soon as he said that one of the guys just about wet his pants and said, 'Man, if he's coming, there's sure enough going to be bloodshed. He is one mean sucker!'

"'Yeah', another guy said, 'I've seen him in action at the bar. The guy's crazy. He'll take every one of us on without a second thought.'

"'You guys are out of your minds,' another said. 'He's just one guy. How bad can he be?'

"'You don't want to find out', the first guy said. 'If you want to stick around that's up to you, but I'm outta here.'

"Several of them started piling into one of the cars like a bunch of scared rabbits and hightailed it out of here.

"The two other carloads of guys didn't know what to do. Finally one of them said, 'If they're that scared maybe there's something to what they're saying about this guy. Maybe we better leave too!'

"'C'mon, you chicken, too?' the driver of the third car asked.

"'Naw', someone responded, 'but I'm not stupid. If you want to take him on, then he's all yours,' he added as he stepped on it and sped off in a cloud of dust.

"Mac, you should have seen it," Len busted up. "My little kid brother was just laughing his head off. He was teasing the last car load of guys. He told them that there was only one car left now for Mac to take care of when he got here instead of three. When he said that, the driver told the rest of them that he wasn't hanging around any longer. He took off down the road with the other guys running after him hollering, 'Stop! Stop! Wait for us!' He slowed down and let them get in and then he tore out of there. Mac, I don't know what you've done to put such fear in them, but I can tell you they weren't gonna take any chances."

"I don't know, Len. I must have put the scare into them all right, but I want you to know that you scared me today. I thought I was back in Vietnam all over again," I said.

I left Len's that day realizing that I hadn't left as much behind as I had thought. My past was very much alive, even though I had done my best to forget through drugs, violence, and running hard. I'd tried my best to run from it, but it had been quietly gaining on me all along. I'd only been a hair trigger away from all the memories and hurt firing off again. I left Len's that day badly shaken — realizing how fragile I really was. I was a delicate time bomb inside, just waiting to explode.

Once a Hog, Always a Hog

• • •

About that time another friend from my past stepped into my life and began an earnest crusade to reform me. Glenn had been one of the only stabilizing forces I had known during high school. He'd stuck with me like glue. We had drifted apart since then, but fate brought us together once again. While I had taken a path that led me into the military and the biker underground, Glenn had taken a more conventional and conservative route. He was in his fourth year of college when he ran into me one night at the road house. Like Len, time and circumstances hadn't severed the bond that had cemented our friendship years before.

Glenn had always provided balance and stability to me when I was enduring a stormy home life during high school. He had been a moderating influence when I began to hang out with the wrong crowd. He was one of the few people I respected and one of the few I would tolerate speaking about my life.

Shortly after we met up again Glenn began to tell me I needed to change my ways. I let him get away with it because I knew he really cared for me. He was smart enough not to push me past my limits, but he didn't give up either. I would think to myself, "What does he know? He's just a square college frat guy who's never been out in the real world. How can he relate to what I've been through?" But most of what he was saying made sense. Besides, in the back of my mind I knew that my lifestyle wasn't getting me anywhere except down a dead-end road. When he continued to encourage me to try to change, I decided I had nothing to lose.

My mother couldn't believe it. One afternoon Glenn and I showed up at her house. He actually got me to get in the bathtub and take a hot bath. He was in there helping me scrub off the layers of dirt and body funk. He had brought some scissors and a razor. He went to work cutting my hair and helping me shave off my beard. I couldn't believe I was actually letting him get away with it. He had always had a tranquilizing effect on me, so I just passively went along with it. When he finished cleaning me up he took me downtown and bought me some new clothes. Man, you wouldn't have recognized me. I was actually clean-cut for a change.

He took me to some of the fraternity parties around the college he attended. He introduced me to a lot of the college women. They were all so naive and innocent. It was like introducing a wolf in sheep's clothing to a flock of compliant sheep. They were all so willing and silly when they'd get drunk at their college parties. I went with the flow and cooperated with Glenn's private crusade because it was an entirely new experience. Besides, Glenn had turned into a real party animal in his own right. He was doing pretty well in college, but he hadn't let his academic responsibilities get in the way of the party scene. He was one of those individuals who had the ability to juggle his scholastic load with an active night life without letting his grades slip. Needless to say, we got into a lot of fights and wild parties together during those few months of transformation. Looking back, Glenn's influence really hadn't changed me that much. It had only introduced me to a refinement of the life I had already been living.

My clean-cut image didn't fit with the role I had played as a roadhouse bouncer. I quit my job, and decided to find something a little more respectable. I applied for a position at a corner drug store working the front counter and stocking merchandise. It wasn't long before the availability of prescription drugs became a lure I couldn't resist. My street smarts and smooth rap were put to good use in winning the favor of the pharmacist. I talked him into providing narcotics for the fictional war wounds I had brought back from Nam. Like being in the college party scene, putting me in that drug store was like sticking an old wily fox in a henhouse filled with plump juicy chickens. In no time I was stealing Demerol and codeine. I was selling the drugs to eager college kids at the parties we attended.

In some ways Glenn did help me clean up my act on the outside; but nothing had really changed on the inside. It was all just a sham — a phony veneer. You could take the pig out of the pigpen, give it a bath, brush its coat, sprinkle it with perfume, parade it around the county fair, and even win some big blue ribbons, but you couldn't take the pigpen out of the pig. Inside, my heart was just as corrupt and polluted as ever. Yeah, I had my new plastic teeth, short hair, and preppie college clothes, but the real Mac Gober was still living behind the facade.

At one of the parties we crashed I met a college sophomore who was attracted to me. She knew I wasn't like the other guys she dated. She found the aura of danger and wildness in me tempting. She was young and innocent and easy pickings.

She was at a party with a big football jock the night I met her. Everyone was drinking screwdrivers and acting giddy. I caught her eye and worked my way over to her, trying to act cool. She could tell I was closing in but let me know in her own flirtatious way that she was willing. I told her to dump the jock she was with. She agreed to meet me the next day.

We started going out a lot and eventually got married. I guess it came with the new territory. It was part of the new and improved image I was struggling to maintain. That was destined to be the worst mistake of her life. I proceeded to turn her life into a living hell. We'd get into the same knock-down-drag-out fights I had known so well as a kid. I had a short fuse. I didn't like anyone jumping in my face, especially some screaming woman. In the biker world if your old lady jumped in your face she got the living daylights beat out of her.

In a few short weeks she informed me that she was pregnant. I went completely crazy at the news. I was cursing and screaming at her like it was all her fault and I had nothing to do with it. I told her I wanted her to get rid of it — like it was just a piece of toilet paper you could flush down the toilet. She didn't want to, but I told her I was going to find a doctor who would do it. I threatened to do it myself if she refused to go to a doctor, and she finally surrendered to my threats. I found a back-alley doctor who performed abortions, but he botched the job. He caused her to hemorrhage. She nearly died. It was the first of nine abortions I would be responsible for.

For seven months we fought each other until our fighting reached a climax one night when she went hysterical and climbed into my face. I exploded and started slugging her and throwing her into the wall. She was screaming and crying and begging me to stop, but I was completely out of control.

"I've had it, you...I'm leaving," I screamed as I slugged her in the face. She hit the wall and crumpled into a sobbing heap on the floor.

"Don't leave," she pleaded as blood dripped on the floor. "Please take me to the hospital," she begged. She was bleeding badly from deep cuts on her arm, but I didn't care. She deserved it as far as I was concerned.

"You asked for it this time," I towered over her, swearing as I kicked her in the side. "You can die right here for all I care," I shouted. "I'm outta here this time. We're finished!" I swore as I turned to leave.

"You're worse than an animal, just like everyone said you were, Mac. You have no heart. You're just dead inside," she sobbed as I slammed the door behind me, leaving her to bleed to death on the floor. Thankfully she managed to drag herself over to the phone and call for help. The paramedics arrived a short time later and drove her to the emergency room to get her stitched up. That was the last time I saw her and it was the first of three failed marriages I blew through.

The bomb that had been ticking inside of me had finally gone off. All the cosmetic attempts to clean up my act had failed. Like I said, you can take the pig out of the pigpen, but let him loose and he'll just return to wallow in the mud. I had about as much hope of going straight at that point as a snowball in hell. Something had gone off in me that night and I knew I couldn't straighten up or stay around much longer.

A restlessness had begun to build in me like the mounting swell of an oncoming breaker. My brothers had become more and more insistent that I come back. They had even crated up my Harley and shipped it to me to whet my appetite. I'd tried to put them off by telling them that things were going well and that my private pot plantation was bringing in some good yields. But the call of the road and the lure of the brotherhood were irresistible. I had grown to miss the feel of the highway wind in my face.

After that final blowout with my wife something changed in my gut. I started pulling away from Glenn and doing more drugs. I still lingered around the university trying to pick up unsuspecting coeds, like a shark circling for the kill, but my time was running out. I was feeling the tug of California calling me back. With the breakup of my seven-month marriage I realized the whole scene fit me like a bad pair of shoes. What little good Glenn had managed to instill in me was rapidly unraveling as I slipped back into my old ways. I couldn't keep a steady job. I started selling more and more drugs to raise money. I started breaking into homes and businesses to steal things to sell on the black market. I broke into a jewelry store and stole some diamonds to sell to a fence. The Tuscaloosa police were doing everything in their power to put me away. They'd haul me in for petty infractions, but they couldn't make anything stick. They wanted me bad, but they couldn't get enough evidence to put me behind bars for good.

After nearly beating my wife to death a few weeks earlier I reached a point where I was completely strung out on drugs. I was taking so much speed and drinking so heavily that I was a mental wreck. I'd try to read something, but the words would just run off the page like sand. I couldn't concentrate or keep my thoughts together. I lived in a drug-induced daze. The paranoia and fear were back, and with them, an oppressive cloud of hate and bitterness, which overshadowed my every thought.

The turmoil came to a head when I walked into my mom's boyfriend's house stoned out of my mind on crank. I found my mom sitting at the kitchen table with a cigarette in one hand and a glass of vodka in the other. Her alcoholic boyfriend was sitting there with her in a drunken stupor. The sorry scene of those mid-day drunks set off an instant rage.

"Why don't you leave this lousy drunk you're with?" I yelled at my mother.

Her boyfriend stood up from the table and screamed right back at me, "Who you calling a lousy drunk, you good-for-nothing scum! You're nothing but a motorcycle hoodlum. You may be dressed different on the outside, but you're still nothin' but a filthy bum," he slurred the words as he staggered out of the kitchen.

"How can you live with that bum?" I asked contemptuously, slamming a clenched fist against the wall. I caught movement out of the corner of my eye just as my mother's boyfriend stepped back into the kitchen carrying an old shotgun.

"Get outta this house you piece of...," he threatened as he raised the double barrel and cocked back one of the hammers.

I was still too fast for him. I swung around with a karate kick that knocked the weapon from his hands.

"Don't hurt me," he cowered in wide-eyed terror as I grabbed him by the throat and slammed him up against the wall. I drove a fist into his stomach, knocking the wind out of him in a gush of air. I came down with a vicious blow to the side of his face, driving him to the kitchen floor.

"I'm going to kill you, you stinking drunk!" I screamed as I proceeded to pound him senseless.

"Stop it, Mac!" my mom screamed. "Stop it, you're killing him!" She tore at my shirt and hair.

I backhanded my mom, knocking her to the floor. Her boyfriend's face and shirt were covered with blood. I picked his limp body up and heaved him through the kitchen window in a shower of shattered glass.

My mom ran outside, with me in pursuit. All I could see was red. I was going to finish off her boyfriend. My mom was on the side of the house kneeling over him as he lay crumpled on the pavement.

"Mac, you're no good!" she screamed. "Look what you've done!"

"Shut up!" I growled as I grabbed her by the hair and jerked her to her feet. I slapped her across the face then backhanded her again.

"Mac, please don't hit me anymore!" she pleaded as blood flowed from a cut lip. "Stop, please stop. Don't hit me," she sighed as she slumped to the ground. I grabbed her hair in a knot and dragged her into the house and tossed her onto the floor crying. I stormed out of the house that day, vowing never to come back.

A couple of days later I cooled off. I called her to see how she was doing.

"Mac," she said in a stone-cold voice, "you've gone and done it this time. Ralph went and called the police. He told them he was pressing charges for attempted murder."

"I know, Mom," I answered in a controlled voice.

"How do you know?" She seemed surprised.

"I've got connections in the police department, that's how," I said and hung up the phone.

The contact on the inside was a college kid I had been selling drugs to. His father worked for the police department. He had a part-time job pushing papers. He'd quietly snoop around when no one was looking to find out what was coming down. Because of the inside information he came up with I was able to stay one step ahead of the cops. I'd been playing this cat-and-mouse game with them for months. I'd made it into a contest. Sometimes I'd leave little notes on my door saying "Sorry you missed me, boys, maybe next time," just to taunt them. I remember one time I was sitting in a restaurant when this detective came in and sat down across from me with a half-smoked cigarette dangling from the corner of his mouth. "You think you're slick don't you? Don't think for one minute we don't know what you're up to, Gober," he said in a challenging voice. "We know what you're doing and when you're doing it, punk. One of these days your luck is going to run out. When that time comes we're going to nail you to the wall. When we do we're going to stick you in a place where the sun don't shine, boy!" the cop said in a threatening way as he ground out his cigarette butt in my plate.

"Don't count on it pig," I said nonchalantly as I shoveled another forkload of food into my mouth.

"We'll see about that," the detective responded as he got up and left.

But my luck had run out this time. The city police put out an all-points bulletin to apprehend me for assault. A patrol car finally spotted me driving on one of the streets near my house and turned on its lights. I floored it and started weaving in and out of traffic to get away. The cruiser giving chase radioed for backup. In seconds several more squad cars with lights flashing and sirens wailing converged on me in a high-speed chase through Tuscaloosa. I swerved recklessly in and out of traffic in a mad dash to escape. I was hitting mailboxes and nearly running over pedestrians. Sixteen patrol cars joined the pursuit and began to close in on me. Finally I tried to make a tight turn down a side street. I skidded across a corner lawn and stalled in front of a drug store across the street. I jumped out of my car and started hoofing it on foot. I was jumping over fences and cutting through yards with the cops in hot pursuit yelling, "Halt, or we'll shoot!"

I was pumping my legs as fast as I could run, over-amping on adrenaline and paranoia. I rounded a corner and turned into an alley. Several cops were right behind me, warning me to stop. I knocked over garbage cans in an attempt to slow them down. I turned into another blind alley and ran dead-end into a chain-link fence. I was frantically clawing my way up when a cop ordered me to drop and put my hands on my head or he would blow my brains out. I let go and dropped to the pavement. I turned around to see half a dozen guns trained on me.

"Down on your face!" one of the cops screamed. "Now! Do it, or you're a dead man!" another demanded.

I dropped to my knees and stretched out on the cement with my hands behind my head. One of the cops handcuffed me behind my back while the others kept their revolvers and scatter guns trained on me. They weren't taking any chances now that they had finally apprehended me.

I started laughing and said, "Don't hurt me, I'm really scared," in a mocking tone of voice.

"You think this is fun?" one of the officers asked. "I don't believe this," another shook his head in disgust.

"You think this is just a big game, putting civilians at risk?" the first officer added.

"Boy, you're in a heap of trouble now. You're doing hard time now!" he said.

"I'm reeeally scared," I taunted them.

They threw me in one of the squad cars and took me down to the police station to book me, get my finger prints, and take my mug shot. I was thrown into a cell to await my hearing.

My getting out was a long shot. That was through a friend whose father was an old war buddy of a respected judge in the city. I convinced my friend to visit me. I laid a heavy guilt trip on him about how Vietnam had really messed me up, and how I was trying to make something out of my life, but that all the pressure had gotten to me. I was having real emotional problems. I shed big crocodile tears and laid it on pretty thick until he really bought what I was saying.

"No problem, Mac. Don't worry. I'll talk to my dad to see if he can talk to the judge," he told me through the glass partition. I'd played so many games and run so many cons I didn't even know when I was lying anymore. Predictably, the scam worked and the judge released me with a very stern warning. He gave me a blistering tongue-lashing and said he didn't want to see me in his court again or he would throw away the key. Of course I promised to be a good little boy and stay out of trouble, but it was all a big lie. I had no intention of going straight or cleaning up my act. I'd already tried that bit and had failed miserably.

When I got out of jail I called my mom. I told her I had been released and was heading back to California. I remember telling her, "You and me both know that I can't stay around here any longer. I don't belong here, Mom. I'm going back to where I do."

There was a long pause on the other end of the line. Finally my mom just said, "Goodbye, Mac," and hung up the receiver.

I called the brothers back in California to tell them I had had it. I was coming home. I was so paranoid that the cops were going to get me that I kept the conversation short. I feared the phone might be tapped.

Overdose

•••

Beating the charge for assault and battery hadn't changed a thing. I was little more than a caged animal they'd let back on the streets. A few days after my release I got into another drunken brawl and nearly killed someone in a fight. I knew by the stern warning the judge had given me that the cops were going to arrest me if I kept breaking the law, so I sought sanctuary in one of the local biker hideaways. I knew I couldn't stick around much longer, so I decided it was time to head back to the West Coast. One of the locals said he'd like to go with me, so we drifted south on our sleds, stopping at road bars and liquor stores along the route to keep ourselves bombed. After several incoherent days of drinking ourselves through Alabama and across Mississippi we pulled into New Orleans. No sooner had we passed the city limits than we were pulled over by the city police. Two outlaw bikers flying their colors and rumbling into town on their chopped hogs was reason enough to signal an alarm. In moments we had attracted half a dozen cop cars. The police could tell we were smashed. They took our I.D.'s and ran a check on them. My buddy's came back first.

His came back with an outstanding arrest warrant for possession of stolen property.

When they informed him that they were going to place him under arrest I said, "You're not going to arrest anybody. We haven't been hassling anyone and we're clean."

"You stay out of this, boy," a police sergeant warned, "or we'll take you in for questioning, too."

Another officer walked over from the squad car and handed the sergeant my driver's license. "Looks like we got ourselves a real live wire here, Sarge. Guy's got quite a rap sheet," he said.

The sergeant looked at the driver's license and then at me and said, "Well, whatd'ya know, Mr. Gober? Looks like we're going to be taking you in with your buddy here for some questioning. Frank, put the cuffs on him," he instructed another officer.

"I said you ain't arresting anybody. We haven't done anything," I protested as the officer reached for one of my arms.

Minutes later five officers had wrestled me to the ground with my arms pinned behind my back and one of their knees in my crotch to subdue me. They snapped on the cuffs, carried me to the waiting paddy wagon, and heaved me inside like a sack of potatoes. They threw me in the wagon loaded with a bunch of winos and gutter bums they'd picked up on their daily street sweep. The insides of the van reeked of sour vomit from one of the drunks who had heaved a belly full of cheap wine all over the floor. Another wino had passed out and was laying in the puddle of puke. They took us downtown to the city jail and stuck us in a large holding tank filled with criminals and drunks waiting to make bail or be called for their arraignment. It was a stinking zoo crowded with petty thieves, pimps, and drunks. Some men were picking the pockets of drunks who had passed out, while others were doing their territorial "macho" bit by trying to intimidate their cell mates and let everyone in the tank know how bad they were. One burley loudmouth tried his routine on me. I kicked him in the groin and elbowed him in the face, which rearranged the position of his nose.

After a few days in the tank for "drunk and disorderly" behavior I was released, once again, to continue my pilgrimage back to Southern California. My companion didn't see daylight for more than a year in the county farm. I don't know how I slipped through the system, but I wasn't sticking around to find out.

My crewcut college look had disappeared over the months as my beard and hair began to grow. I'd discarded my stretch Levi's and loafers. I was back into my grubby biker clothes and faded blue jeans jacket. Another bar fight had removed my dental work, leaving me with my two pointed fangs protruding from my upper gum.

My daily diet of drugs and criminal activity had created a state of perpetual paranoia. I feared being arrested at any moment and sentenced to some county chain gang or state prison. I was alone, disjointed, and completely lost. All I could focus on was the need to get back to the brotherhood. It was all that I had left. At least the biker underworld could provide a way for me to drop out and hide from the dark specters of fear, which were closing in around me.

Finally I made it back to San Diego, after punching it across the Southwest on black coffee, white cross, and my Harley Davidson. I pulled up to the clubhouse that morning with bloodshot eyes looking like pinpricks and a mind burnt to a crisp. I'd been wide awake on that long-haul run for nearly three days. I looked like I had just stepped out of *Night of the Living Dead*. I walked into the clubhouse that day completely fried.

My old buddies were surprised to see me but glad that Big Mac was back. They were sitting around the room, passing joints and breaking open some bricks of pot from a new delivery when I stepped in. Ratman looked up from a pile of grass he was sifting and handed me a freshly lit joint. "Want a hit, Mac? It looks like you could use one. No offense, man, but you look like a road kill, buddy."

"Thanks, man, I could use one," I said. "I feel like a truck ran over me and backed up to see what happened." I chuckled wearily. Everyone else busted up.

"I can dig it, man," a big guy named Moby, said. "It's sure good to see you ol' buddy. We was getting kinda worried about you. Thought you weren't comin' back."

"It's been a real bad trip, man. I just couldn't do the scene back there. It was getting so bad I couldn't turn around without the pigs hassling me."

"Things are going to happen now with Mac, the Maniac back," Ratman flashed a sly grin and sucked a long drag off of a glowing joint.

"We're going to party now," Moby added.

"Party, party, party!" the rest broke into a chorus.

"Far out, man," I said. "You aren't going to get any arguments outta me."

I quickly slipped back into my old pattern of dealing drugs, fighting, prostitution, stealing, extortion, rape, and raising hell. I was as crazy as ever and willing to do anything. In short order I started acting as one of the club's enforcers, taking care of business when drug deals went bad and customers didn't pay up. But even that began to sour as my need for drugs increased. I started busting drug deals when they were going down and stealing the drugs and money to support my habit. As a result, two contracts were taken out on my life. Guys who did that sort of thing had a short life expectancy.

I was as crazy as before, but I wasn't the same. I'd reached a point where I had become a sociopath capable of any act of violence, any act of perversion. I was dropping so much acid that reality had melted into one hallucinogenic distortion. I was living in constant paranoia — fearing the late-night knock on the door or a knife in the back from a member of a rival biker gang. I was a walking war zone, a human hurricane poised to hit at any moment. I was constantly looking over my shoulder and changing my appearance by shaving my head or changing my beard.

I was taking more and more drugs in an attempt to bend reality and escape the turmoil and confusion inside. I'd sit around the clubhouse, what we referred to as our church, and tear pages out of the Bible to roll joints with. I was snorting endless lines of coke to the point where I wasn't even getting off anymore.

That's when I started sniffing angel dust, a white crystal powder called PCP. It catapulted me into another world of mental distortion. My mind was so messed up that I lost track of time and space. The combination of drugs and perversion had so warped my behavior that I was turning into the sickest degenerate you could imagine. My unpredictability and instability finally reached a point that even my biker brothers were repulsed by where I was heading and the sick things I was doing. Even they didn't want to be around me anymore because I could not be trusted. The only thing that mattered to me was drugs, drugs, and more drugs. The only thing I lived for was a way to numb the nightmares and phantoms that tormented my soul.

I had degenerated to the point where I couldn't even think straight. My mind was a kaleidoscope of fears and twisted hallucinations. I was completely useless. I couldn't even take care of myself. A daily overdose of drugs and alcohol had fried so many brain cells I was a walking zombie. The fabric of my mind had become so frayed that it had finally snapped. I was no longer any good even to my brothers.

Within a year of my return I found myself locked in a wooden barn owned by an old Mexican who had taken me in. I had gotten to know the old man through some of my drug deals when I first ran with the club. He and his wife owned a little truck farm nestled in a box canyon west of San Diego. It was tucked away and hidden from view — a quiet green oasis in the midst of the parched foothills. They liked it that way because it gave them a chance to be by themselves. It also afforded him an opportunity to grow his crop of marijuana. I'd grown close to the old man. In a strange way he reminded me of my granddad back home. Orteze was gentle and kind and weathered from years of sun and toil.

When I was first running with the club I had gone out to buy some of his quality grass. I spent hours talking to him and listening to the stories he would spin of his Indian ancestors and their ancient ways. He had a certain unrefined wisdom that made me think. It was a wisdom of this world, but it carried enough grains of truth to make me pause and consider what I was doing with my life. We'd sit together on his porch smoking joints. I would feel a separate peace in his presence and escaped with stories that carried me far away to distant times.

When I finally went over the edge I had nowhere else to go except to his farm. My old lady had called Orteze to ask him to come and get me. She didn't know what to do with me and was afraid I was going to kill myself. He came in his beat-up pickup. He carried me back to his farm and made a place for me in his barn. At that point I was completely gone — self-destructive and suicidal. I'd turned into a ranting, raving lunatic. I resembled a rabid dog in its death throes more than a human being. If I had been an animal they'd have put me to sleep. If the authorities had found me, I would have been stuck in a straitjacket and confined to a padded cell in an insane asylum for the rest of my life.

Poor old Orteze didn't know what to do except lock me in the barn and keep a watch on me while I struggled through my drug deliriums. I'd gone mad. He'd stand outside watching me through the cracks in the wooden siding. He'd see me writhing on the barn floor, convulsing and screaming from bizarre hallucinations and terrifying flashbacks I was having of Vietnam. The torment inside my head reached a point of such insufferable agony that I would pound my head against the wall to get it to stop. I would punch the weathered boards until my knuckles were bloody and raw. At times I would fall into a fitful semicoma between reality and fantasy. At other times I would cry out with bloodcurdling animal-like screams — loud inhuman wails. For two weeks I floated in and out of a world of warped reality. It was a hellish time of demonic terrors and twisted nightmares.

My old lady came out to check on me after a few days. Orteze thought it would do me some good to let her in. When Orteze let her into the barn I grabbed her and took her prisoner. She begged me to let her out, but I held her hostage and wouldn't let her go. I didn't know who she was. I was beating her and throwing her around the barn, thinking she was trying to get me, like all the other specters haunting me. Orteze called to me and pleaded, "Man, don't hurt the lady, Mac. She's tryin' to help you. She's your friend, like me." I heard the words like they were echoing down a long black tunnel and for a brief moment my thoughts registered. I saw his face through the slates and he came into focus and I came to my senses.

Orteze would try to soothe the torment and talk me back to reality. During lulls in my torments, his wife, Mary, would bring me a plate of hot beans and tortillas. She would push them under the barn door. Orteze would come in when I had quieted down to give me water and try to get me to eat. He would comfort me and tell me that it would be all right, but I was little more than a babbling idiot. I was a mental and emotional basket case. Orteze would sit with me and I would cry like a wounded little boy — gut-wrenching sobs that seemed to well up from deep within my soul. I would tell him of the horrible things I had done in Vietnam and here at home. I would tell him of the people I had hurt and the lives I had destroyed. Looking back, it seemed that I had a compelling need to tell someone — to unload the garbage of my soul. He would sit and listen. I would look at his old weathered face and see the face of my granddad.

After two weeks without drugs, I calmed down enough in that crude detox to lie exhausted and immobile on a bed of straw. I was so very afraid of what I would do. I had taken so many drugs. I had gone the limit and cheated death so many times I didn't think I would survive. I was no good to anyone — no good to my brothers, no good to myself. I wanted desperately to escape, but I didn't know any way out of my personal hell.

Curley concentrated on the spoonful of heroin, heating it with a Zippo lighter until the contents liquefied. When it was ready he picked up an old syringe from the coffee table, placed the tip of the needle into the contents, and carefully drew back the plunger, drawing the potent liquid into the syringe.

I sat on that threadbare sofa mesmerized by the bizarre ritual taking place before me. I had just smoked a joint laced with powdered heroin and was drifting in and out of never-never land as I stared through blurry eyes at Curley's performance. It had only been a few days since my old lady had picked me up from the barn. I was back on the streets, pushing it to the limits again.

Curley handed the loaded syringe to his old lady and pulled his belt from his jeans. He ran the tip through the buckle and inserted his arm through the loop until it was around his upper arm. He cinched it tight until it had constricted his circulation. He flexed his fist a few times and slapped the hollow of his arm to pump up the veins. He carefully looked for a good one to inject. His arm was black and blue from the tracks of previous hits. When he found a vein he clenched the end of the belt between his teeth to keep the pressure on his arm tight and reached for the syringe. He held it up in the dimly lit room and flicked it a few times with his middle finger to discharge any bubbles. He carefully depressed the plunger until a drop of fluid appeared on the tip of the needle.

I sat there in a trance watching the strange death dance. Curley carefully placed the needle point on the bulging vein and tapped it gently with his finger until it penetrated the flesh. He pulled back the plunger until it registered a trace of blood, then slowly depressed it until it was empty. He quickly laid the syringe on the table, released the pressure of the belt, and flopped back in the overstuffed chair to await the oncoming rush.

"Here it comes, gang," Curley said just before he started to gasp for air. His eyes rolled back and his mouth gaped open in a startled death mask. We sat there stunned for a moment, thinking Curley was enjoying his rush, until he started to turn blue. We realized he had overdosed. His girlfriend started screaming and shaking him, yelling for us to do something. I was suddenly jolted to my senses by the situation. I pulled Curley up and started slapping him, telling him to wake up, but it was too late. He had OD'd on smack.

The experience was overwhelming. One minute he was there, and the next he was gone. Once again I was brought face to face with the death of a friend. I was floored by the realization of how fragile life was and how close I had come to death — how intimately I had courted it for so long. I remember looking around the room when some of the brothers came to get Curley's body and asking myself, "How did I get to this place? What happened to bring me to this place?" At that moment of finality I knew that I had to escape somehow.

Just As I Am
• • •

I was terrified of what I would do or what would happen to me next. I felt like an unseen specter of death was stalking me. I knew I was careening hopelessly out of control — heading for a dark chasm from which I would never escape. I knew I had to get out or I would soon be like Curley.

I called my mom and told her a big story about being down on my luck — how I was really struggling to straighten out my life like when I was hanging out with Glenn. I told her I would be okay if I could just get some money to buy some clothes for a job. But in the back of my mind, as messed up as I was, I was still scheming to get money for more drugs.

I called Orteze to ask him for a lift downtown to the Western Union office to pick up the money my mother agreed to wire. I was so messed up I couldn't even ride my bike. I just couldn't control my body. I'd start shaking or lose my balance as things would go out of focus and melt before my eyes.

Old Orteze came to get me and drove me downtown in his pickup. He pulled up to the curb and let me off in front of the Western Union office. He said he would wait for me. I climbed out and walked across the sidewalk toward the front door. The office was filled with people waiting for their cash to come through. A long line snaked out the door and down the side of the building. I walked to the back amid the curious glances of the other people in line. A few shifted positions and moved away. One elderly lady let out a disgusted gasp and covered her nose with a handkerchief. Another woman turned around to stare and I curled my lip in a snarl, like I was going to bite her head off.

I was a pitiful sight in my filthy jeans, black biker boots, chains, and faded cutoffs. I just stood there passing gas out loud and spacing out in my dark sunglasses. My scraggly hair was down to my shoulders. My hairy beard twisted in all directions.

The line slowly inched forward until we were through the front door and into the lobby. I was standing there spacing out when I noticed this little guy outside coming down the sidewalk handing out a piece of paper to each of the passers-by and people standing in the line. One by one he would offer them the piece of paper. They would take one look at it and toss it onto the sidewalk. The wind was blowing the scraps of paper around like confetti.

I finally got up to the window and told the clerk, "I'm here to pick up some money my mom wired from Tuscaloosa."

The clerk looked at me matter-of-factly and said, "I'll need to see some I.D."

I handed him my tattered driver's license. He looked at the picture, then back at me and said, "Wait here, I'll be right back." He turned around and walked through the back door, leaving me stranded with a long line of disgruntled customers behind me. I stood there for a few minutes waiting for the clerk to come back, watching the hands of the clock pass time. I was getting paranoid because he hadn't returned. I thought he might be calling the police or something. I was starting to sweat in that stuffy office and felt like I better get out.

Just then I turned around and noticed that skinny little fellow still moving down the line passing out those pieces of paper. The people would look at the paper and draw up their faces or simply crumple the paper into a ball and drop it to the floor. The man finally got to me and handed me one.

He never said a word. He just walked up and quietly offered me the leaflet. I took it from him. He stood there for a moment looking at me — my shaggy head of hair with my fangs hanging down — like I was a perfectly normal human being.

He just smiled and turned to go, leaving me at the head of the line holding this funny little scrap of paper between my fingers. I looked down and tried to focus on the words, but the print was too small. I brought it up to my eyes and stared at the heading. "JUST AS I AM...," read the print. "So what," I thought to myself. "I know who I am." I tried to toss the leaflet aside, but it was stuck to my grungy fingers. I tried to flick it off again, but it just hung there, stuck to my thumb.

I was so dirty and sweaty from the body filth I had accumulated that I was like a piece of living flypaper. My personal hygiene had deteriorated to a point worse than that of a hog, and I just didn't care. There were times I would be standing in a line at a store and I would just relieve myself where I was standing. I would let it puddle on the floor through the holes in my old motorcycle boots without giving it a second thought. If I was riding down the freeway and got a yellow jacket stuck in my neck or some other bug that had splattered into my hair, I would leave it in there just to get a reaction from people. I'd be sitting around with my buddies and I'd pick up a spider crawling down the wall. I would put it on my tongue and swallow it just to freak them out. I didn't care what people thought — the cruder the better. I'd pick my nose and belch and make ugly faces at people just to gross them out. There would be times I would go into a crowded restaurant. I would walk up to a table of strangers and break wind or make faces at them until they'd get up to leave. Then I would sit down and eat the food they left on their plates. Once I was at a party and some chick asked me what my sign was, expecting me to say "Libra" or "Capricorn" or something. I just looked at her and said, in dead seriousness, "Perverted. I'm perverted. That's what my sign is." And I was.

So I'm still standing there looking at this little piece of paper glued to my thumb, thinking to myself, "I know who I am. I'm the filth of the world...aw, who gives a flip anyway?" I tried to flick the scrap of paper away once again. But it wouldn't come off. I tried rubbing it between my thumb and fingers, but it was just stuck like tape.

I was starting to get nervous as the paranoia began to build. The clock was still ticking away. The clerk still hadn't come back with my money. I was worried that he had made me or had gone to call the police. I was getting ready to explode, and that stupid little piece of paper was really ticking me off.

"What the—." The piece of paper was hanging on for dear life as I flicked it again. "What's going on?" I asked myself as I held that little piece of paper out for a better look. That's when the smaller print began to come into focus. "There's such a crazy idea today that people have to give up all their bad habits before God can accept them. Most people think that they won't go to heaven unless they go to church and do good works. But God accepts you just as you are. He loves you right where you're at. Most people do not believe that God can accept them just as they are. They think they are too bad for God to love them or they have done too many sinful things, but the Bible says in Romans 5:8 that 'God demonstrates His own love toward us, in that WHILE WE WERE STILL SINNERS, Christ died for us.'" I stood there reading those words, totally distracted from the delay. It was like they were leaping off that little piece of paper and right into my heart. I read on, "Be honest with yourself right where you are. Be honest with yourself right now. Confess that you need a Savior right where you are. God loves you more than you will know. 'For God so loved the world that He gave His only begotten Son, that whoever believes in Him should not perish but have everlasting life' (John 3:16). Bring your misery, your pain, your guilt to Him and He will do the rest. Jesus died for your sins. Why? So you would not spend eternity in hell. Why? Because He loves you so much. He took your place on the cross to pay the penalty for your sins. He died in your place so you wouldn't have to. All you have to do is be honest with yourself and confess your sins before God just where you're at. Ask Jesus into your heart and repent. Turn from your wicked ways, and see if Jesus will not forgive you...."

I stood there at the front of that line, dumbstruck by those simple words that pierced me right to my heart. I saw that word "honest" and it hit me right between the eyes like someone had fired a gun point-blank in my face. I had never been honest in my life. I'd never been honest with myself or God. I had spent my life running from the truth. I had never thought about heaven or hell; even when my granddad had told me about Jesus I had not taken it seriously. I had mocked God so many times. I had made jokes about Jesus. Jesus Christ was nothing but a profanity to me. I'd be in a bar with my friends, all of us bombed out of our gourds, and I would stand on top of the bar and pretend I was Jesus hanging on the cross. I would stand up on the counter shouting, "Hey, someone come and pull the nails out of my hands; they're killing me!" People would laugh and shout catcalls. They'd come over and pretend they were taking the nails out of my hands. I'd fall off the bar with my feet still dangling from the top of the counter and I'd scream out, "Hey, you forgot the feet! You forgot the feet!"

I read those words "Just as I am" and I thought to myself that it couldn't be true. I'd done so many wicked, cruel things in my life, even God couldn't forgive me. It just had to be a bunch of garbage.

I was standing there running these questions through my head when the clerk returned. "Mr. Gober, here's your money," he said as he adjusted his horn-rimmed glasses with the tip of his finger.

I snapped out of it; I rolled up the piece of paper and stuck it in my pocket, thinking that it would make a good piece of rolling paper for later on. I grabbed my money and left with old Orteze. I tried to put the words

I had read out of my mind, but they kept coming back. I started asking myself what would happen if it was all true and I would have to stand before Him one day and give account for all the evil things I had done.

Still, I couldn't get off the track I was on and soon all the money my mom had wired was burned up on drugs. Two weeks later I walked through the front door of a drug addict's house where I often hung out. As I stepped in the door I looked down and saw a pamphlet lying on the floor. I picked it up and wondered what it was. I sat down at the kitchen table and started to read. It referred to all the amazing prophecies in the Bible that had come true — how the coming of Jesus had been prophesied hundreds of years before His birth and how over three hundred specific prophecies had been miraculously fulfilled. It went on to tell how God had spoken of the last days and of His Second Coming, and I thought to myself, "If He was right the first time, He must be right about His coming again to judge the world." I sat there thumbing through that pamphlet, thinking how strange it was that I was running into all this God stuff.

Just then I heard this groaning in the next room and someone let out a raspy cough.

"Hey, what's going on, Mac?" Digger said as he staggered down the hall and over to the refrigerator to get a beer.

"Not much, man," I said as I flipped through the pages of that pamphlet.

"Boy, did I have a rough one last night," Digger added. "Got pretty tweaked, man. It was a heavy night," he said as he popped open a cold beer and stared at me with bloodshot eyes. "Hey, what do you got there?" he said as he looked at the pamphlet I was holding.

"I found this lying by the front door," I said, flashing him the pamphlet.

He was rubbing his eyes and propping himself up against the counter. "Oh, that," he said. "This ol', fat, black woman was passin' them out this morning and POW! I hauled off and hit her in the mouth. That pamphlet fell out of her hands."

I couldn't believe what he had just said. I was thinking to myself, "What kind of woman would dare come into a neighborhood like this and pass out Bible stuff?"

I left Digger's house later that night, but I couldn't leave behind the nagging knowledge of that precious black lady who had gone door to door in that rough neighborhood passing out those tracts. "What kind of love could someone have to risk her life like that?" I kept asking myself.

For two weeks that dear old black lady never left my thoughts. I couldn't get her out of my mind. I kept asking myself what kind of love she must have had to leave the safety of her church to come down to a rough neighborhood like that just to tell people about Jesus. All the perverted things I had done kept going around and around in my head like a broken record. I kept thinking that if all the things in that pamphlet were true about Jesus coming back to judge the world I was in serious trouble. I couldn't turn those thoughts off. They just kept flashing on and off in my head like a warning light.

I thought of my granddad and what an old fool I had thought he was. I remembered the way he talked to Jesus. I thought, "Maybe my granddad was right after all. Just maybe he was the wise one, and I've been the real fool all my life." I wanted to end the pain and turn it all off, but I didn't know how. I had no one to talk to.

A few days later I came home abut two in the morning. I slowly plodded up the stairs to my little apartment with a heavy heart, my shoulders feeling like I was carrying the weight of the world.

I opened the door and stepped into my dark apartment. I reached to turn on the light when I was suddenly spellbound by the image of Jesus hanging on the cross in the corner of the room. I stood there staring when the revelation suddenly struck me that He was hanging there just for me. I heard this distinct voice saying to me, "Mac, I love you." I knew it was the voice of Jesus telling me that He died just for me. I stood there staring at the cross in amazement, when an overwhelming sense of peace came flowing over me like warm waves of heat. I had never felt anything like it. "Mac, I love you." The words came to me again. My knees weakened and I sunk to the floor. I began to cry uncontrollably. Hot tears were streaming down my face. I looked over at the image and said, "No, Jesus, You couldn't love someone like me. How could You love me?" I could see Him loving good people and honest people and godly people like my granddad, but I couldn't comprehend a love that could love me.

"But, Mac, I do love you," the words came back again.

I tried to remind Him of all the evil, perverted things I had done, but His words cut me off. "But, Mac, I love you," Jesus said.

It was all so real, but I didn't know what to think. I hadn't been drinking or doing drugs for a couple of days, because of the sobering impact of those gospel tracts. I didn't know if I was just hallucinating or having some strange dream. I had to know. "Lord, I don't know if this is all real...if this is really happening to me...if I'm really hearing You. I've got to know for sure," I pleaded. I reached around to flip on the switch when an intense light flooded the room. A holy fear came upon me. I knew it was the presence of God. I looked back and saw the word "GOD" stamped in large bold letters on the wall, like they'd been stamped there by a branding iron. I knew for the first time in my life that He was real and that He had died for me. I began to cry with a loud voice, "Oh, God, please don't let me go to hell. Please God, forgive me. I'm sorry for all the things I have done. Please have mercy on me!" I shuddered with groans that rose from deep within my soul as hot tears flowed down my face.

I just let it all out before Him. I didn't know any eloquent King James prayers — "Oh Lordest, thou knowest, that I needest to confesseth my sins with my mouthest." I just cried out a simple prayer for Him to save me, and forgive me, and cleanse me. And I felt His love wash over me with waves of cleansing. It felt like all the joys of humanity had been compressed into one rapturous moment. I fell over in my bed steeped in His love. I lay there for hours sobbing until I cried myself to sleep.

Born Again

• • •

I flopped my legs over the side of the bed and sat up. The room was dark. I stood up feeling lighter than air. Coming home the night before I had felt like a thousand pounds of anchor chain were welded to my body. An enormous burden of sin had lifted from my heart, giving me a freedom I had never before experienced.

I turned to see if the image of Jesus hanging on the cross was still in the corner of my room, but I couldn't see anything. I was blind. I rubbed my eyes, but nothing happened. The amazing thing was I didn't care. I was so overwhelmed with happiness, I just didn't care. I staggered around the apartment bumping into things. I was saying, "Lord, I know I've been bad. I don't care if You've blinded me, because I have been so bad. I'm just thankful that You saved me!" And I meant it!

I was laughing and talking to God like He was in the room with me. Just then I remembered lying on my bed the night before pouring my heart out to Him. I remember crying out to Him and asking for two things: "God, if You let me live, please help me to find my mom so I can tell her how sorry I am for all the horrible things I have done to her. I've got no right to ask You for anything, but I'm begging You to help me get things right. And, God, please help me to help young people so they don't turn their backs on You and end up the way I did. I don't know how to do any of this, but I'm asking You to help me."

I groped my way into the bathroom and over to the sink. I turned on the faucet and splashed some water on my face. I reached up and pried open one of my eyelids and saw my big hairy face looking back at me from the mirror. I was even more ecstatic. There I was like the Abominable Snowman grinning at this big ugly face with two fangs and puffy eyes and I was filled with joy. I had cried so hard for so long my eyes were swollen shut. The feeling of joy that overwhelmed me cannot be put into words. I was filled with an overwhelming sense of love.

The knowledge that God had met me and saved me was something I couldn't comprehend, but I knew it had happened. I knew He had met me that night. Years later people would question me, "Now, c'mon, Mac, did you really see a vision of Jesus on the cross in your room that night? Did the room really light up like you said?" And I would tell them that it happened just as I said. God is my witness. You don't just get up one morning, put on your shoes, say, "I think I'm gonna become a Christian today," and suddenly change. He knew what it would take to get my attention. He knew when this old sinner was ready. Maybe it was like Paul's experience on the road to Damascus. Some people don't need for God to crack them along the side of the head with a two-by-four to get their attention, but He came to me in the loneliness of that room to touch a desperate heart in the way He knew best.

He knew how much I despised religion and how much I had mocked anything to do with Jesus. I would read the comics in the newspaper and see this little cartoon of a bearded guy in sandals and a robe holding a sign reading "Repent!" I'd rip up the paper and go into a rage. He knew what was needed to reach down into my cold, stony heart that night and save me. He knew I had to reach the "gutter most" — that I needed that strange little dude at the Western Union office to hand me that piece of paper and that dear old black lady to leave that pamphlet for me to find. He knew when I was ready to listen — when I was ready to receive His great love toward us all.

I was so happy it felt like my chest was going to explode. I wanted to hug somebody. I wanted to shout it out and tell somebody, anybody, what had happened to me. I changed my grubby clothes, found the cleanest pair of blue jeans and shirt I could find, and headed down the stairs from my apartment. When I stepped into the morning sun I couldn't believe my eyes. It was like everything had changed — like it was a whole new world. The sky was bluer, the trees were greener, the sun was brighter. I was bubbling over with joy. An indescribable feeling of love and compassion had overcome me. The love of God had swept over me and filled my heart to overflowing. It was just pouring out of me, like Jesus had climbed inside and was showing me how much He loved mankind. I just couldn't contain it. I felt like hugging everybody. I had a big smile stretched across my face. To this day people will say to me, "Mac, you've got one of the biggest smiles on your face." I tell them that Jesus put it there and I can't help it!

I walked down the sidewalk feeling like I was going to burst when the thought came to me, "I know, I'm going to find me a church!" I realized it was Sunday morning and I knew from my days with my granddad that Sunday was the day religious people went to church. I got into my old clunker of a car with the windows down and the breeze blowing through my hair and headed down the road in search of a church.

Now you have to understand that I was about as theologically ignorant as they come. I mean I didn't know what a denomination was or what born again meant or the difference between an epistle and an apostle. All I knew was that I was saved and I loved God. I just wanted to share it with others who felt the same way.

Well, I was scooting down the street when I saw this church with a parking lot full of cars so I pulled into the lot, parked my old car, and headed for the door. When I stepped through the door they were right in the middle of the service and everyone turned around to see what the disturbance was. You could have heard a pin drop. I could almost read the expressions on the startled faces: "Oh, God, he's come to rob us!" Everyone was sitting there with a tense expression on their face like they'd been dipped in starch and glued to their pews. I thought their heads might snap off as I walked down the aisle. I was beaming from ear to ear with my fangs sticking out. I was waving and nodding and sticking my hand out. People were looking at me like they had been sucking oats out of a gas pipe and saying to themselves, "What do you want?" I walked up to the front of the church and found an empty seat in the front pew. The preacher was standing dumbstruck behind the pulpit looking like he was on the verge of a coronary. I looked up at the pastor with that big toothless grin on my face. He just stood there looking back at me like he'd just seen someone come back from the dead. He cleared his throat and tried to regain his composure to continue with his sermon. Well, the service didn't last long. It was one of those churches where they started at eleven o'clock sharp and ended at twelve o'clock dead. But I sat there like a kid in a candy store enjoying my own personal revival. When the preacher finished his sermon and started to close the service I stood up and walked forward to the altar. I was pretty ignorant of traditional church services, but I could remember when I was nine at my granddad's church when people would go forward after the message and get prayed for. So I just stood up and walked forward in complete innocence. The preacher looked down at me like, "On, no, here it comes!" I just walked up there with tears flowing down my face and reached out with my two big hands to shake the preacher's. My heart was so tender. I looked him in the eyes and said, "Brother, I'm comin' home." And I could almost hear him thinking, "Oh, God, I hope it's not my home." I wanted to tell somebody I loved them. I wanted to go up to one of the little old ladies who reminded me so much of my granny and hug them, but I was afraid they'd keel over right on the spot. I stood there for a few moments with the preacher, then turned around. The place was empty. Everyone had abandoned ship as quickly as possible, leaving that preacher alone to deal with me.

I was on a real spiritual high. I was saved and free and going to heaven. I just couldn't take the joy of it all in. I was driving down the freeway later that night on my chopper, basking in the good news, when I looked up and saw that big, sixty-foot cross all lit up on top of El Cajon. I remember having to pull my Harley over to the shoulder because the waves of gratefulness came crashing over me. I started to pour out hot tears of joy again. All those years living in San Diego, doing drugs and raising hell, I had passed that cross many times, but I had never noticed it. But that night I looked up and it struck me again what Jesus had done for me. I just broke down and cried like a little baby — this big motorcycle biker hunched over the bars of his chopper with traffic shooting by, crying his eyes out.

For weeks after that I would notice crosses everywhere. I'd be cruising down a street and see a cross on some church steeple poking through a hole in the trees. I'd be rumbling down the interstate and see a cross etched in the side of a mountain. I'd be sitting down in a restaurant and look across the street and see a cross on a corner. Each time the Holy Spirit would speak to me and say, "That's right, Mac; you're looking at the right thing now. Don't ever forget what that cross means and what Jesus did for you. Keep your eyes on the cross and follow Me. I am the way."

I had the strongest desire to go home to find my mom and get things right, but I didn't have any money and dealing drugs just didn't seem right. I rode down to the unemployment office a week after I got saved and waited in a seat for my name to be called. I sat there for a couple of hours, smoking cigarettes and waiting as patiently as possible. I was still smoking pot and sucking cigarettes because I just didn't know any better. Finally my name was called and I was taken to a desk for an interview by some bored social worker.

I sat down in the chair next to her desk. She gave me the onceover like she was thinking, "Sorry, we don't have any positions open right now for outlaw bikers."

"Well, Mr. Gober, what can I do for you?" she inquired matter-of-factly.

"I need a job, real bad, ma'am," I replied.

"What skills do you have?" she asked.

"I'm willing to do anything. I'll dig ditches, I'll wash dishes. You just name it," I responded. "Whatd'ya have?"

The woman just sat there stalling for time, thinking to herself, "Nobody is going to hire this dirt bag." She was thumbing through some forms like I was taking up her precious time.

I bowed my head and whispered a simple prayer under my breath: "Oh, Lord, please help me to find a job. You know I want to do the right thing."

No sooner had I finished than she turned to me with a warm smile on her face and said, "Well, Mr. Gober, this must be your lucky day. Do you think you could work with aluminum siding? I've got a position open. It's minimum wage, but it's something."

"Sure, Ma'am! I can do anything," I grinned my big toothy grin.

"Well, you'll have to go over there and talk to the foreman first," she added.

"No sweat," I said. "I'll head right over there."

I rode my chopper over to the plant and went inside the front office. I asked for the name I was given.

"Hey, Frank, there's a guy out here wants to talk to you about that job," the guy behind the counter yelled to the back.

"Be right there," a voice sounded from the rear of the makeshift office. I looked around the room and noticed a little silver cross tacked to the wall above a desk cluttered with stacks of paper. I knew right then it was going to be okay.

A moment later a man stepped out of the back room and told me to follow him. We went outside and walked around the plant for about forty-five minutes while I shared with him what had happened. Since I had gotten saved I had such a compelling desire to share my experience with everyone.

The man listened carefully and finally said, "Well, young fella, you seem bright eyed and you sure got a good attitude. I can use anybody who's willing to work hard."

"Well, your lookin' at the right man, sir. I won't let you down," I promised.

Later that afternoon I headed over to the clubhouse to share the good news with my biker brothers. I thought they would be happy for me. That's one of the funny things I soon found out about bringing Jesus home with you. I mean, you can drag anything else home and there's no problem — Buddha, some weird cult, some tripped-out guru — and no one seems to mind, but bring Jesus home and you might as well have brought home the bubonic plague.

I remember stepping into that smoke-filled living room with half a dozen guys supercharging grass through a shotgun barrel. They all looked up and saw me standing there with this enormous grin on my face.

"What've you been doing, Big Mac? Looks like you got a good hit off of something," Ashtray coughed.

"Man, I found Jesus," I said innocently.

"You found what?" Ratman responded. "Are you trippin' out again, dude?"

"A couple of nights ago Jesus came into my room and saved me," I said. They were all staring at me like I had two heads or something.

"Aw, man, don't tell us you're a Jesus freak," Ashtray said in a disgusted voice.

"You'll get over it," Ratman added.

"Man, I'm tellin' you, He's real. I'm not trying to lay some trip on you," I said.

"You overdose on something?" Ashtray asked, looking at me like I was one of those pod people who just stepped out of the *Body Snatchers*. "You'll come down after awhile."

"No, I ain't overdosed on nothin'. I'm telling you that Jesus is real, and He loves you very much," I said. "I'm telling you like it is, man. You should have been there. This bright light came out of nowhere and filled my room and God spoke to me."

"Right," Ashtray said in a sarcastic voice. "God spoke to you? You've really twigged out this time brother." He shook his head in disgust and went back to smoking his dope.

Well, they didn't want to hear any Jesus stuff. Some of them were uptight and ready to lay into me, but my reputation for having a whiplash temper cooled their willingness to press it. I just told them that I loved them but that I needed to go back and find my mom. I just needed to work and save up some money to go back home and clear up some things with my mom.

After three months at the aluminum plant I had saved enough money for the trip back home. I packed my few belongings and saddled up my cycle. I broke the news to my brothers that I was leaving. I kidded around with them and told them, "Hey, I'll be back. Once a biker, always a biker. Right?" Some of them actually wished me well. Others were razzin' me and giving me affectionate "center punches" for a send-off. A few disgruntled ones told me I was just copping out with this Jesus trip and they would come after me if I didn't come back. I told them all again that I really loved them, and I meant it, because that overwhelming sense of love that had so engulfed me was still rushing through me like a river. I had to learn who I could talk to. It wasn't acceptable to talk about it openly in front of the guys. I told them that Jesus loved them, too, but they shined it on with awkward jests and told me, "Yeah, yeah, yeah, Big Mac, that's all we've heard out of you. You've been singing and smiling and acting goofy for three months with this Jesus thing."

First Love
•••

I made my way back across the Southwest to my roots in Alabama. I had a driving urge to go home and find my mom and tell her how very sorry I was for all the hurtful things I had done to her. The memories of my dragging my screaming mother across the floor by her hair and smashing her over and over in the face sent stabbing pains of remorse through me that I needed to heal.

No sooner had I arrived in Tuscaloosa when an army of police descended upon me like a swarm of locusts. They wanted to know if I was back to cause trouble. I looked one of them right in the eyes, and with a big smile plastered on my face said, "Officer, you're not lookin' at the same guy you think I am. I met Jesus Christ, and I've come home to find my mom and serve the Lord. You're not going to have any trouble from me." My answer took the police completely off guard. They never expected me to say something like that. If I had told them to get outta my face or to mind their own business they would have been prepared, but telling them that I had found Jesus was completely disarming.

I had raised a lot of hell in those parts, but I came back determined to make restitution. I remember going to a jewelry store I'd broken into and stolen a lot of diamonds from to ask for the owner's forgiveness. I had ripped off a lot of people and owed money to handfuls. One by one I went to each of them and told them with tears in my eyes, "I want to ask you to forgive me for what I did to you. I want you to know that if it takes me the rest of my life I'm going to pay you back every dime." The amazing thing was that it totally blew their minds — every last one of them. People I'd done dirty and stolen from would look at me asking them to forgive me for all the dirty rotten things I had done. They'd get all choked up and start crying themselves. Even stuffy old shopkeepers would stand there with this hairy brute asking for their forgiveness and their eyes would well up with water. They'd clear their throats and try to keep their composure. Most of those folks were so moved by my tender spirit and sincerity that they would say something like, "Mac, if I can do anything to help you just let me know."

I started looking for some work and found a job as a topographical technician — i.e., rod holder for one of the county maintenance crews. I started earning some honest money and began to look around for my mom. I'd lost contact with her since I had left and had to do some searching to find out where she had moved.

I remember the day I rode up to this small house my mom was living in. I walked to the front door, pulled back the screen door, and knocked a few times. A couple of moments passed before the door swung open and I greeted my very surprised mom.

"Hi, mom, your boy has come home," I said softly.

"Oh, Mac!" she exclaimed with tears in her eyes.

I stuck out my arms, and we hugged each other in a long embrace. She pushed herself back and ran her fingers through my bushy beard. "My baby, my baby," she sobbed. "What's happened to my baby?" she asked with tears running down her face.

I stood there in the entryway all choked up and said, "Don't worry, I'm going to be okay. Your baby's going to be just fine."

We stood there crying and comforting each other for a few moments, then I took her hand and dropped down to my knees. I was looking up into her face when I said, "Mom, I want you to know that I love you. When I was away, Mom, I found Jesus and He changed my life. He's shown me how to love and live again." She had big tears rolling down her cheeks and dropping to the floor as she stood there looking down at my own wet face. "Mom, can you find it in your heart to forgive me for all the bad things I have done to you and said to you?" I asked. She didn't say anything. She just held me tight against her as she sobbed with joy.

We must have cried for hours during that joyous reunion. When we had regained our composure I said to her, "Mom, will you go to church with me?" She looked a bit surprised. "Mac, I haven't been to church in years. I...I don't have anything to wear."

"Aw, mamma, you don't have to get all dressed up. Just come with me," I asked.

That next Sunday we went to a big Baptist church. It was full of people and my presence created quite a stir that morning. Many of those people had known me in high school and knew what kind of life I had fallen into. When the sermon was finished I got up and walked to the front. My mother followed me to give me support. I just wanted to ask for God's forgiveness again and get baptized. I just wanted to do what was right. I walked down to the front with my mother while hundreds of eyes watched us. I was crying again and so happy. I'll never forget the well wishers who thronged around us that morning. People were huddled around me shaking my hand, pumping it up and down, and saying things like, "Welcome back, Mac." "It's good to see you, Mac." People were standing there like they were waiting to meet a celebrity or something, telling each other, "I knew him when he was...I knew him when he did...And look at him now. He's got such a twinkle in his eyes!"

Little by little I started to grow in the Lord. I was still so young and innocent. I was filled with an effervescent happiness. I was so happy, smiling constantly. I was still smoking cigarettes, but God was cleaning me up at His own pace, gently dealing with my unrefined innocence.

I met a girl when I got back to Alabama and she ended up moving in with me. At that point I was so biblically ignorant, I thought that if I loved her and treated her right and didn't hurt her like I had done to so many women in my past it was okay with God to live with her outside of marriage. You have to understand that I was so new in the Lord and ignorant of so many things. I just hadn't yet been convicted by the Holy Spirit. Thank God, He catches the fish first before He cleans them. He was loving and gentle and brought me along in His time.

One Sunday morning at the church I was attending the pastor started preaching this hellfire and brimstone message about the evils of fornicators. I sat riveted to my seat, spellbound by the fiery message thundering from the pulpit. I was thinking in the back of my mind, "Those awful fornicators must be pretty wicked!" Well, I didn't know what in the world a "fornicator" was. I had some vague idea it was one of those gladiators who killed people in the coliseums in the old days. The pastor never explained what they were. He just talked about adulterers and other sinners who were going to go to hell if they didn't repent and get right with God.

After the morning message I walked up to the pastor and shook his hand. "Pastor, that was sure some sermon this morning! Those fornicators must be some really bad dudes!" I said.

"Yes, son, they're going to burn in hell if they don't give their lives to Jesus," he said.

"By the way, pastor, what are them old fornicators exactly?" I asked innocently. I was about as sharp on spiritual matters as a bowling ball. "What did they do that made God so mad at them?" I asked.

"Son, that's when a man sleeps with a woman and they aren't married," he answered sternly and I thought to myself in a panic, "Oh, no, he's looking right through me. He knows every hidden thing in my life!" I was cut right to the heart and thought, "Man...Oh, God, I've got to take care of this 'cause I sure don't want to go to hell!"

I rushed home and ran through the front door, startling the young woman who was staying there.

"You gotta get outta here!" I said in a panic. "We ain't fornicatin' no more."

She looked at me like I had just lost my marbles and said,

"Forni-what'tin?"

"It don't matter what it is, but God don't like it and we ain't doing it no more," I said. "You gotta leave."

I was young, but my heart was right. I just wanted to obey Him and do what was right. All it took was a word from the Lord and I was ready and willing to respond.

I was filled with that first love of salvation — so simple and happy, so uncluttered and uncomplicated. I was still pretty rough around the edges, but I started bathing regularly and putting on clean clothes. I just wanted to serve Him and do what was right.

One afternoon I was coming out of this corner market where I had stopped to get a Coke. It was a sweltering summer day. It was one of those days when you could see the wavering heat vapors rising off the asphalt. I was walking across the parking lot to this old clunker I was driving when I noticed a little, gray-haired lady hunched over in a car. I thought she might have suffered heatstroke. It was so hot under that blazing sun that the heat waves were rippling off the top of her car. I saw that old lady sitting in there baking and I thought to myself, "I'll be a Good Samaritan and see if she needs some help." I walked over to the car and reached for the door handle to open it when she looked up and saw this big hairy monster standing there trying to pull open the door. She started screaming in terror and pulled back on the door. I was trying to explain to her that I only wanted to help, but all she could see was this hairy hulk with two fangs trying to drag her out of her car. Just then I was cracked along side of the head, "Get away from my mother! Get away from my mother!" a lady screamed as she swung her purse around again to give my head another wallop.

"Man, I love Jesus," I said as I backed up, covering my head with my hands.

"I don't care who you love, you look like an animal," the lady shouted.

"I wasn't going to hurt her," I said. "I just wanted to open the door and give her some fresh air."

Well, I left with a real heaviness in my heart. The words from that woman had really cut deep. I didn't want to hurt anyone. I didn't want to scare people or gross them out anymore. I decided I'd better make some more changes. I found a barber shop. I went in and sat down in the chair.

"What can I do for you?" the barber asked as he snapped the apron and draped it over my shoulders.

"I wanna haircut," I told him.

"You just want a trim?" he asked.

"No, sir, I want you to cut it short, like that guy over there." I pointed to a clean-cut-looking guy sitting in another chair down from me. And cut the beard off too, while you're at it," I added.

"Are you kiddin'?" the barber asked.

"No, sir, I'm serious," I answered.

I started going to a Nazarene church and growing more and more in the Lord. I was young in the faith and burning with fervency. I wasn't too theologically sound, but in my youthful zeal I probably got more accomplished without knowledge than I would have with a head cluttered with theological roadblocks. I was on fire and burning with a passion to tell everyone about Jesus. I had bumper stickers plastered all over my car telling people how God loved them and Jesus was coming back. I'd realized early on that it wasn't any good trying to convert churchgoers or preaching to the choir. I also noticed early on that sinners weren't exactly beating down the doors to find God, so I looked for every opportunity I could to tell people about Jesus. Man, I was ready to win the world!

I was about to drive my poor ol' mom crazy with my zealousness. She'd tell me this religious thing was going too far and I was turning into a fanatic. I was always reading the Bible and singing to myself. She'd stop me and say, "Mac, you're reading that book too much. It's going to drive you crazy if you keep it up! You need to calm down and be more sensible about this thing!" But I would tell her that I was really crazy before and Jesus was the One who had brought me back. I'd ask her how the truth could hurt you. She finally moved out of the house we shared to a little apartment because it was just too much Jesus for her to handle at that point in her life.

A couple of years later she called me and said, "Mac, son, it's real! Jesus is real, just like you said!" She'd finally gotten a good dose of genuine Jesus.

I started visiting the roadhouse where I had worked as a bouncer to talk with some of the familiar faces who hung out there. I ran into that one old boy who had ridden with me as far as New Orleans a couple of years before — the time we got busted by the police. When it had happened I had blamed him for getting me in trouble and vowed to kill him if I ever ran into him again. Now there I was, full circle, sitting at that rowdy roadhouse, a changed man talking to this guy about Jesus. I struck up a conversation with him and spent the evening talking to him about what had happened to each of us since we had parted. Gradually the conversation steered its way toward God. I eventually told him about my salvation and how Jesus had met me in such a powerful way. I turned it around and began to challenge him about his personal need for Jesus.

"You need to get saved, man. You need to give your life to Jesus," I told him.

"I know, Mac," he said.

The only problem was, I didn't know what to do after that. I was like an inexperienced salesman who didn't know how to close the deal. All I could think of after telling someone about his need for Jesus was taking him to see the pastor. So about midnight I took my friend over to the pastor's house and knocked on the door. A light went on, a crack appeared in the door, and the pastor peeked through the crack. He said, "Something wrong, Brother Mac?"

"No, pastor, I got one out here," I half-whispered.

"Got one what?" he asked as he covered his mouth and yawned.

"A sinner. He wants to get saved," I replied with a big grin on my face.

He looked at me with a bewildered look, then looked down at his watch and said, "Brother Mac, it's after midnight."

"I know. Ain't it great?" I said. All I could think of was, "everyone oughtta be excited about someone meeting Jesus."

"Well, all right, Brother Mac. Wait here. I'll get my robe and slippers and I'll be right with you," the pastor said.

We followed the pastor across the cold grass of his lawn to the church, which was next door to his parish. He unlocked the church door and turned on the lights. We went down to the altar and knelt down. The pastor began to pray with the man to receive Christ. Well, it was like getting saved all over again for me. It was so thrilling knowing that I had helped another wretch like myself find Jesus.

Well, the next night I was standing outside the pastor's door about two in the morning. It took him a little longer to answer the door this time, but when he finally did he cracked it again and said in a groggy voice, "What's wrong this time, Brother Mac?"

"Nothin', pastor. I just got another one out here," I said.

"You got another one?" The pastor's voice sounded surprised and a bit disturbed at the same time. "Wait, just a minute," he added.

The pastor went through the ritual of getting his robe and slippers, leading the procession across his lawn, opening up the church, and leading the newly saved man through the sinner's prayer. I was so ecstatic I felt like I had just been launched into space. I mean, I was really peaking on God. It just fueled my desire to go back and find another sinner and help him find his way.

A few days later I got a call from my pastor.

"Brother Mac," he said in a serious-sounding voice, "I would like for you to meet me in my office on Thursday. I'd like to have a little chat with you, if you don't mind."

Well, that telephone conversation sent a pang of fear stabbing through me. I had instant flashbacks to earlier days when I had been summoned to the principal's office for something I'd done wrong. Boy, was I nervous. I mean, I was sweating bricks.

When the time came to meet with the pastor, I walked into his office and took a seat in front of his desk. I felt like I was sitting in the witness box for a cross-examination.

"Now," he said as he cleared his throat! "Mac, we've been meeting quite a bit here lately."

"Yes, sir," I replied sheepishly.

"Man, I've got to tell you that you're looking pretty good, son — a real handsome young man," he said, trying to put me at ease.

I smiled real big. "What did you wanna see me about, sir?" I was a little unsure of what to think.

"Mac, I think you've got it now, son," he said as he held up a set of keys. "Look, here are the keys to the church. You can just come and use it any time you want. You don't need me to lead all those people to the Lord. It's time you started doing it. It doesn't seem like you are having much of a problem finding them."

I couldn't believe what he was saying. It completely floored me. I slumped in that chair and started crying with joy. I was so moved that this godly old man would trust me. Nobody had ever trusted me, and now he was offering me the keys to the church. It was a sacred trust that I felt so honored to have been given. I felt like I was the pope or something. I left that office on cloud nine, twirling those keys around on my finger and tossing them up in the air.

That little church started to come alive. People were accepting Jesus and whole families were getting baptized. All I could do was beam from ear to ear and try to whistle as best I could without any front teeth. I was still simple and unformed in my Christianity, but I had an infectious love for Jesus and a burning passion to win people to Him.

One Sunday morning I walked into the church and one of the church elders, old Brother Rufus Hammond, approached me and said, "Mac, some of the church members would like to have a word with you." I followed him over to a corner where a dozen men and women circled around me. I was standing in the middle of them, feeling like I was about to get ambushed, when Brother Rufus opened his mouth.

"Brother Mac, I'm serving as the spokesman for the rest of us," he nodded toward the others and gestured with a wave of the hand. I didn't know what to think. Maybe they were fixin' to ask me to leave the church.

"Brother Mac, I'm speaking for this here group. Auugh, umph," he cleared his throat. "We want to ask you to forgive us," he said as big tears suddenly formed in his eyes.

"Forgive you for what?" I asked.

"Brother Mac, this church has been sittin' here for years now. We've been doing little more than warmin' the pews. We got comfortable in our salvation and have just been playin' church for years. When some of us were younger this church was on fire for Jesus, but we just got caught up in our own lives and the cares of this world. We kinda put God on the back burner. We forgot what we were saved for, Brother Mac. Some of us have been 'in the way' for many years now. God has showed us that we need to get out of the way so He can move," Brother Rufus said with a chuckle. "Ever since you began comin' to this church we started asking some questions and doing a little soul searchin'. You kept bringin' people here every Sunday. Some of them didn't look so good or smell so good but you went out and got them. You told them about Jesus, and we could see the changes taking place. We could see God working in your life. Well, it convicted us, Brother Mac. It reminded us of what we once had. We looked and saw you with that big smile and those big blue eyes twinklin' all the time. We could see how much you loved Jesus. Mac, we lost our first love, and we want it back. You've given this little church back a fire, Mac. We want you to know that we're goin' to be going out and invitin' people too from now on! We want God to keep moving around here. We want to move on with Him!"

I looked around at all those precious old people saying, "Yes, brother, that's right," with their heads bobbing up and down like those little toy dogs they stick in the back of cars. And my heart felt like it was going to burst with joy.

Turning Point

• • •

As the first couple of years of my salvation passed I left my infancy in Jesus and began to mature in Him. I also took my first tentative steps into ministry. The one thing I didn't lose was my zeal for Him and my hunger for the things of God. It was a time of gradual growth and spiritual shaping in the Master's hands. It was also "the day of small things" and humble beginnings. I was learning to walk in simple obedience and to trust Him at His Word. It was not a time without the predictable tests and trials to my newfound faith, but His mercy was sure and His faithfulness constant. He carefully guided me through the many mine fields the enemy placed in my path. He kept me from falling during the dark night of the soul and the voices from my past, which were calling me back to California. Through the times of testing He taught me to trust Him to be my provider, and He taught me to keep my eyes fixed on Him.

About this time I told a Southern Baptist friend of mine about a week-long conference that was going to be held in Tulsa, Oklahoma. I asked him if he would like to go with me. They were going to be ministering on the power of the Holy Spirit in the believer's life.

That first night we were standing in a sea of people. Oral Roberts was ministering on the Holy Spirit and the Spirit of God started falling on people all over the auditorium. Hands were shooting up all around me and people were praising God. All of a sudden my Baptist buddy started speaking in tongues. He turned to look at me like he wanted to say, "Hey, this isn't what I came here for!" It was a little too much for his theological conditioning to handle. I was so open to whatever God wanted, I just stood there praying with my hands lifted up. All of a sudden it was like warm waves came rushing over me. I started speaking in tongues, too. Talk about being zapped! It was for real — spontaneous and genuine. The Holy Spirit just spontaneously engulfed me.

On the last day of the conference I was wandering around the front lobby of our hotel, checking out the tables piled with literature, when I noticed a booth with a sign above it that read, "Do you have a testimony?" I stared at the sign and thought to myself, "Boy, do I have a testimony!" I walked over to the booth, sat down in front of this woman, and started sharing with her what had happened to me — how Jesus had reached into that dark pit I was in and pulled me out. After about five minutes she stopped me and said, "Don't say another word. Come back later this afternoon. I want to take your picture and record what you've just told me on a tape recorder so we can put it in one of our magazines."

"Well, whatever the Holy Spirit wants, that's what I want," I told her. I came back later that afternoon like she said and she was all excited.

"Mac, would you be willing to share your testimony with everyone before Brother Roberts ministers tomorrow? I've got to check to make sure we can do this, but your testimony is so powerful I just know it will bless people. We've never done this before, Mac, but I feel so strong about this in the Lord."

"Well, I just wanna be used, ma'am. If I can help someone else I'm willing."

"I'll check on this and call you back as soon as I find out," she said.

The next morning she called my hotel room and told me that it was okay. She informed me to be ready that afternoon. She said I would have five minutes, which seemed then like an impossibly long time.

Man, talk about being scared. Butterflies were squirming around in my stomach. You have to understand that I had come to this conference to be ministered to, not to minister. I was still a babe in the Lord. Oh, I wanted to serve Him, but I wasn't looking for a big ministry or to get my name in lights — let alone to share with five thousand people. I wasn't clamoring to be somebody or build some little kingdom for Brother Mac; but God must have looked down, seen my tender heart, and felt it was time to take me off the proverbial shelf to put His message of grace to work.

When the time came I was sitting on the stage as nervous as a Chihuahua. One of the ministers gave me a brief introduction and turned to gesture me forward. I felt like the whole world was watching me as I stood to my feet and walked across the platform. I stepped up to the podium with five thousand pairs of eyes watching with anticipation. I felt like a sixth toe as I scanned the mass of people; but as soon as I opened my mouth the Holy Ghost fell and a surge of boldness swept over me. Six minutes later thousands of people had risen to their feet, weeping and clapping and praising God. That huge auditorium sounded like crashing waves as thunderous ovations reverberated throughout the hall. I had never experienced anything like it. I stood there for a moment awe-struck, when the minister stepped up to the microphone and announced that they were going to take a fifteen-minute break before Oral Roberts started to minister.

No sooner had I stepped down from the platform than I was thronged with people wanting me to autograph their Bible. People were pressing in around me with tears running down their faces. People were streaming out of their seats from all over that massive auditorium and making their way down to the front where I was standing. Pastors were coming up to me asking me to minister in their church. Full Gospel businessmen were sticking cards in my pockets. People were wiping their eyes and trying to shake my hand. The whole experience was a bit overwhelming. I was still standing in the corner of that auditorium shaking hands and giving people my address when Oral Roberts began to minister.

During the conference I made friends with this older Methodist lady who kept bumping into me throughout the week. Evelyn Alexander and I seemed to take an instant liking to each other. I started calling her "Mom" and sat with her throughout the conference. After I finished sharing she came up to me with several hundred others and told me that the Lord had showed her that I was the reason she had come to the conference. It was the first time she had been to anything like it. She told me that it had changed her life and given her hope for her two sons. That meeting with Mom Evelyn would blossom into a lifelong friendship in the years to follow.

I left that conference with a fresh vision in God. It was a pivotal point in my Christian walk — a turning point that would lead me down the path the Lord had destined for me. I returned to Birmingham, Alabama, knowing that God, in His infinite wisdom and perfect timing had orchestrated that week and used it to confirm His call on my life. I didn't know what it all meant, but He had birthed a confidence that He would direct my steps and lead me into the ministry in His times and seasons.

I moved in with my Uncle Joe and Aunt Ruth and got a job selling vacuum cleaners. I was selling Rexair Rainbow vacuum cleaners from door to door, but my heart really wasn't into the sell as much as the contacts I began to make with my customers. I would be invited into their homes and find myself on my knees demonstrating the benefits of owning a brand new Rexair Rainbow. The conversation would eventually drift toward my salvation experience. In short order I was thrust into "vacuum cleaner evangelism," and people were accepting Jesus because of a vacuum cleaner contact. I was working hard at my job and winning people to Jesus, but times were tough and most of my contacts didn't have the money to shell out for a new vacuum cleaner. Jesus didn't cost them anything, but the Rexair Rainbow was too much.

As a result, my finances started drying up. I remember going through a real struggle wondering how I was going to make ends meet and if I would ever go into the ministry. I remember telling God, "Father, if you want me to get another job and do that for the rest of my life I will, but if you want me where I'm at I'm going to need a miracle." I was on my knees praying that prayer when the phone rang. "Mac, I want you to come over. I know this may sound crazy, but the Lord just spoke to me to give you my credit card to help you pay for gas," the voice of a church member sounded on the other end. No sooner had I laid down the receiver when the phone rang again. "Brother Mac, listen, I was just praying and I felt like the Lord wanted me to give you some money," another said. Neither of the callers had known of my need or of my prayer, but God had intervened and spoken to their hearts. God had shown me that He didn't want me to leave and find another job. My life was on track and He was showing me, in no uncertain terms, that in spite of the testings of my faith He was still in control.

Days later an older couple called me. "Brother Mac, my wife and I would like you to come over to our house for dinner if you could. We have something we want to share with you," the man said.

We were sitting down at the table for dinner when the lady said, "Mac, we are going to go out for a little while. Okay?"

I nudged the chair back and stood up, thinking they were going to excuse themselves from the dinner table for a few moments. "Where are you going?" I asked. "Well, the Lord told me to do something when you were in our home a few weeks back," the man said. "Mac, remember when you were here and you demonstrated that vacuum cleaner? Well, we didn't end up buying it, but we had never been around anybody who loved Jesus so much and had such a pure heart. We used to go to church, but we got hurt during a church split and drifted away. You didn't have any way of knowing this, Mac. We used to give regularly to a missionary. The Lord spoke to us and said you're a missionary here in our own backyard. This country needs people like you who aren't ashamed of Jesus. Now, even though you didn't sell us that vacuum cleaner, you really touched our hearts and we want to do something for you." That night they took me out to a shopping mall and bought me a brand new suit. They also gave me an envelope with some money in it and it turned out to be the exact amount I would have made on a commission if I had sold them the vacuum cleaner.

I left that night with mixed emotions. On the one hand, I was really encouraged that the Lord had shown Himself to be my provider. But on the other hand, I felt this undercurrent of guilt tugging at my heart. I felt like I wasn't being honest with my employer. In my heart I was just using that Rexair Rainbow to get my foot in the front door so I could end up witnessing to people about Jesus.

God was moving behind the scenes and between the lines of my life. I knew He had placed a call upon my life for ministry, but I didn't know what it all meant or the direction that ministry would take. I did know that I had a passion to testify to the things the Lord had done in my life and a burning desire to reach young people with the Gospel.

When that call came the skies hadn't parted. There were no angelic choirs singing the "Hallelujah Chorus" or supernatural bolts of lightning streaking from the heavens, but He had planted an undeniable witness in my heart that He was preparing me for His service. I hadn't been to a seminary or a prestigious theological school, but I loved His Word. I had not been molded by tradition or structured by ritual, but I knew of His power to save. I hadn't been raised in a church setting or been groomed by religious professionals, but I knew

He had saved me for a reason. I hadn't even come from a good home or a wholesome background, but I was born again and was a new creation in Him. I had been the scum of the earth, a vile human being, but He had redeemed me to show others the power of His love and the glory of His grace for even the worst of sinners. I knew that the Bible said, "God has chosen the foolish things of the world to put to shame the wise,...the weak things...to put to shame the things which are mighty;...the base things of the world and the things which are despised God has chosen, and the things which are not, to bring to nothing the things that are, that no flesh should glory in His presence," and that gave me confidence that He could even use someone like me. I was just trying to be faithful in the small things and wait patiently upon His timing.

One day I was driving down the road outside of Birmingham, heading for another Rexair appointment, when I saw a hitchhiker thumbing a ride up ahead. I remember that at the time I was thinking I was going to have to tell my boss I had to quit. My heart was no longer into selling vacuum cleaners. I didn't know what to do and was feeling frustrated at the lack of direction in my life. It was in that frame of mind that I pulled my car over and picked up the hitchhiker. He told me he was living on the streets and needed a ride into Birmingham to pick up his next dose of methadone at the treatment center. He'd been on heroin for several years but said he was trying to kick the habit.

We struck up a conversation. I started sharing with him about how the Lord had delivered me from a life of drugs and perversion. About a half-hour into our ride he asked me to pull the car over and let him off.

He said this was as far as he was going, but I think the Jesus thing was just too much for him to handle. I pulled away with him visible in my rearview mirror, thinking to myself, "Lord, I wish I had had a little more time with him."

The very next day, when I got into Birmingham, I stopped off at a restaurant to get a bite to eat. I was minding my own business eating my supper when the same hitchhiker walked in, sat down at a booth, and ordered dinner. He was digging into his burger when I walked up and sat down across from him. He looked up from his plate like he had just seen a ghost.

"Now, then, I think we need to finish that conversation we were having," I said. He sat there with a mouthful of food and a dumb expression on his face.

I ended up taking the guy home with me to give him a place to crash for a few days until I could find a place for him to stay. I called around to different churches to see if there was a home or ministry that took care of guys like him. I was finally referred to the local Teen Challenge center downtown. I had read *Run, Baby, Run* and *The Cross and the Switchblade* and had heard of the Teen Challenge program, but I didn't know much about it. I did know they didn't use methadone to heal addicts but relied instead on the power of Jesus Christ. They had a very successful ministry with drug and alcohol addicts and worked a lot with street people. I knew I wasn't doing much good shuttling him down to the methadone center for his daily fix while working full time to scrape by a living selling Rexair Rainbows.

I called the center and got hold of the director, Dan Delcamp. I explained the situation. He told me to bring the guy over for an interview. When we sat down in his office I didn't pull any punches with the guy and told him like it was. I told him that he needed to quit whining about all the bad breaks he'd gotten and stop making excuses for his life. I told him it was no use trying to con a con. I'd been out on the streets, too. I'd done the drug scene, so I knew where he was coming from. Dan didn't say much; he just sat there listening while I exhorted the guy. At the end of the counseling session the guy said he'd decided not to enter the program. He didn't want to make any commitments. He was just looking for a place to kick back and get a free ride.

I drove the guy downtown to drop him off. I was just getting ready to pull over to the curb when I suddenly turned into an alley. I looked at the guy and said, "Before you go I want you to know that Jesus loves you. But you've got to want to help yourself. I want you to bow your head and pray with me before you go." I led him in a sinner's prayer then turned to him and said, "Okay, get out." He climbed out of the car and slung his backpack over his shoulder.

"Listen, one more thing before you go," I said as I leaned over in the seat and handed him a card. "Take this. If you ever want to get serious and decide you really do need the Lord's help to beat this thing call this number any time, day or night."

He nodded like he wasn't interested and shut the door. I was soon to learn, though, that God had brought that reluctant hitchhiker across my path for a reason. He had brought him across my path because He had other plans for my life.

The next day, I was packing up my things to head to Texas to see Mom Evelyn. I really didn't know where to go from there, but I knew that my time was up selling Rexair vacuum cleaners. Vacuum cleaner evangelism had seen its day. That's when the phone rang.

"Mac, this is Dan over at the center. What're ya up to?" he said.

"I'm fixin' to leave," I answered.

"Oh, yeah? Where you plannin' on going to?" he asked.

"Well, I don't know for sure, but I thought I'd head out to Texas to visit a close friend," I said.

"Hey, Mac, before you go, could you stop by the center for a few minutes? I'd really like to talk to you about something," he said.

"What about?" I asked, not sure what he was leading up to.

"Why don't you wait until we can talk face to face, okay?" he said.

"No problem. I'll swing by on my way out of town," I answered.

When I got there Dan took me into his office and had me take a seat in front of his desk. "Well, Mac. I'll get right to the point. I'd like you to pray about joining the staff here at the center and becoming the resident director. I watched you in action with that hitchhiker the other day. I feel like you've got the anointing and street smarts to really reach these guys. Whatd'ya say, Mac?"

Man, it was like a bomb went off in my head. I couldn't believe my ears. I didn't know what to say. I mean, I was totally blown away. First God had brought me together with that hitchhiker, which had led to the visit to the Teen Challenge center. Then God had stopped me at the last moment from going to Texas. I mean, my car was loaded, the tank full of gas, and I was heading out the door when the phone rang. I was beginning to learn the simple truth that "God is never late." I sat there stunned for a moment and then started to cry.

"Anything wrong, Mac?" Dan said with concern in his voice.

"No, no," I tried to regain my composure. "This has to be God, Dan. I was going to Texas to preach in the private home of some friends. After that, I didn't know where I was going. I was getting to the end of my rope and didn't know what He had planned for me after Texas. But I guess He had other plans," I chuckled.

"Well, Mac, before you decide I think it is only fair for me to tell you that besides your room and board we can only pay you a hundred dollars a week," he added, apologetically.

"Man, I'd pay you a hundred dollars a week just for the opportunity to do what I love the most — ministering to hurting young people!" I said. "This is all too much, man! I'm about down to my last buck, I don't know what the Lord has in store for me, and all of a sudden the door opens. You're gonna let me live here for free — no rent, no utilities — and give me my three meals a day, and you're tellin' me I can minister all I want to a captive audience of men?"

"Well, that's about the long and short of it, Mac," Dan smiled a knowing grin.

"God is really good, isn't He?" I said as I stood, tears running down my cheeks, and gave him a big hug.

Beauty and the Beast

• • •

Since the sermon that convicted me about forni-
cation, I had made a personal vow not to date until I
knew it was His perfect will. I wanted the right woman
at the right time for my life. I wasn't into missionary
dating. I wasn't hopping from church to church like I
had a bad case of "Galvation." My salvation was real. I
didn't want the distraction of dating until I was
grounded in my spiritual life and had my priorities
focused in Him.

I'd actually put the whole issue of dating on the
back burner. But as the months ticked by I found
myself in my prayer closet more and more asking the
Lord if it was time to date. I had committed my natural
desires to Him. I was perfectly willing to wait for his
permission, but I knew I didn't want to be single. Each
time I would entreat the Lord with "Lord, I don't want
to be lonely for the rest of my life. Is it time for me to
date?" He would give me a definite no in my heart. I
secretly feared that I was going to end up like one of
those eunuchs I'd read about in the Bible. Time after
time I appealed to Him, until a day when I didn't get

up from my prayers feeling an uneasiness in my spirit. He hadn't said yes, but He hadn't said no either.

A short time later I went to visit my mother in Tuscaloosa and invited her to an Assembly of God church in the area. I wanted her to be around the baptism of the Holy Ghost. When we were there I was looking around the congregation. I saw this woman singing in the choir and did a double take. She was the most beautiful girl I had ever seen. I couldn't wait until the service was over so I could check out the situation — do a little detective work and find out if she was wearing a wedding ring. When the service ended I looked over to the choir, but she had already left and was kneeling at the front altar praying with another woman. "Oh, I like that!" I whispered to myself.

I tried to be as inconspicuous as possible as I took a peek at her left hand. Sure enough, she didn't have a wedding ring on. I pulled aside one of the ministers to ask him if he could give me her phone number, and he did.

I found out that her name was Sandra. For the next two weeks it became a personal crusade of mine to get in contact with her. I would set my alarm each morning and call her before she went to work, but no one ever answered the phone. The lack of response only made me more determined to reach her. I started setting the alarm earlier and earlier until I was calling at three in the morning, but still no one answered. Finally I started calling late at night, but still no answer. I was thinking to myself, "This girl is the prayingest girl I've ever heard of, or she doesn't live at this number anymore, or I was given a bum number."

Out of desperation I called my minister friend back and told him that I couldn't get through to Sandra. He told me to call her sister's house because she might know where Sandra was. As soon as I hung up I dialed the sister's number. "Hello, my name is Mac Gober. I'm the resident counselor at the Teen Challenge center in Birmingham. I visited your fellowship a few weeks ago and was trying to reach your sister, Sandra. I've had no luck getting through with the number I was given so one of the ministers gave me your number."

"Well, she's not living at her place right now," the voice answered. "She's living with a lady who just went through a painful divorce and is having a hard time. She's trying to comfort her for awhile," she said.

Man, my heart did backflips. "What a woman of God," I thought. "If it's not too much trouble, ma'am, could you give me her number?" I asked.

"Sure," she said with an upbeat voice.

I finally put through the long-awaited call and got a hold of Sandra. I was pretty anxious at that point. I mean, I was a three-time loser at marriage, was thinning out on top, and had tried already several times to get hold of her. At least I had a new set of dentures, which softened my appearance and made me presentable. My palms were sweating and my mouth was bone dry when I started dialing Sandra's number.

"Hello," a voice answered.

"Ah, yes," I stumbled, "may I speak to Sandra? My name is Mac Gober." I was so nervous it felt like my heart was going to jump out of my chest from the adrenaline rush.

"Hello," this sweet voice sounded on the other end.

As soon as I heard that voice I regained my composure and introduced myself. I asked Sandra if she had noticed me sitting toward the front of the church when I visited. I told her I was the one saying things like "Amen, brother. Preach it, brother. Praise the Lord."

"Yes," she said. "I do remember a visitor that Sunday. We don't get many visitors — especially enthusiastic ones like you. Weren't you the blond with an older woman with you?" she added.

I told her that the person she had seen was me. For the next hour and fifteen minutes I proceeded to pour out my entire testimony. I didn't hold anything back. I'd waited for God's timing and now that it had come I wasn't into playing games or leading her on. During that long-distance testimony, I told Sandra that I'd been an outlaw biker, been through three failed marriages, and been responsible for nine abortions. I explained how God had stopped me in my tracks and saved me. I wanted to be up-front with Sandra so she wouldn't find out later if she decided to date me. I could just see her walking into some place, bumping into a friend, and saying, "I've met this wonderful man by the name of Mac Gober," then watching the person grab his throat gagging and coughing and keel over from a stroke right on the spot because he knew about my past.

When I finished telling her about my testimony I ended the conversation by saying, "Listen, Sandra, I want you to know that the man I was just talking about died in 1974. The guy talking to you right now is a new creation in Jesus Christ. That old Mac Gober doesn't exist any longer, and he'll never hurt another human being. I'm being as honest and open with you as I know how to be, Sandra. The past is behind me and I'm only living for Jesus and the future from now on. After hearing what I've just told you I wouldn't blame you one bit if you didn't want to see me. But if you can find it in your heart, I would love to meet you in person and take you out to dinner to get to know you better." When I finished saying all this my heart was in my throat.

I was planning on going up to Tuscaloosa for an appointment the following weekend, and I asked Sandra if she would go out with me when I got into town.

As I waited anxiously for a response from the other end of the line, I tried my hardest not to get my hopes up or set myself up for a big letdown. I really expected Sandra to tell me to get lost after all the garbage I had just told her about my past. That moment of silence was almost as unbearable as being strapped to an electric chair waiting either for the switch to be thrown or for a last-minute reprieve from the governor.

"Yes, Mac, I would love to go out with you," Sandra answered.

Man, I almost went through the roof when I heard those simple words. "You...You would?" I said, almost in disbelief.

"Yes, call me when you get into town and we'll go from there," she said with sincerity in her voice.

The following weekend we met and had a wonderful time. We felt an instant attraction for each other. Now, I don't want to come across sounding superspiritual about our relationship, but Sandra had a deep love for Jesus and only desired His best for her life. There was nothing superficial or phony about her faith or her convictions. She was a real woman with real desires and needs, but she wasn't about to sacrifice her integrity or virtue on something outside of God's will. She had made a personal covenant with the Lord at an early age not to get caught up in the dating game or in chasing boys through high school. She didn't want a relationship until the Lord, in His wisdom and perfect timing, brought the right man into her life.

When I got back to my room that night in Birmingham I dropped down to the carpet on my knees and prayed, "God, if I never see that woman again...if I never see her for the rest of my life, I want to thank You for lettin' me see that there is a difference between a woman who just goes to church and a woman who sincerely loves You with all of her heart."

I'd been around my share of church girls who were more interested in dating and finding a boyfriend than in having a relationship with Jesus Christ. I wasn't really interested in that scene. I just wanted a woman who loved the Lord as much as I — someone who could be equally yoked with me. I didn't care if she was tall or short or fat or thin. I wasn't as concerned with the outward appearance as I was with the condition of the inner being. Finding a woman like Sandra, who was as pure of heart and in love with Jesus as she was — and as stunningly beautiful to boot — was just too much for me to take.

I remember kneeling on that floor and praying to the Lord, "Even if I never get to see Sandra again, at least I know what it is like to meet a spirit-filled woman who's in love with You!"

I found out later that Sandra had called her mom when she got home from that first date and told her that she had met a man sold out to Jesus. She shared with her all of my testimony. Her mother was elated that Sandra had finally gone out on a date with someone. I mean, here's a woman who had never had a boyfriend, had never gone out on a date, and had never kissed a guy!

Two weeks after our first date Sandra called her mother again and said, "Now, Mom, you know that young man I told you about?"

"Yes, darling," her mother answered, fearing the worst.

"Mom, I'm going to marry him," she added.

"Marry him?" her mom was surprised.

"Mom, I've told you and Dad before that I wasn't going to date anyone I couldn't marry," she said.

"But, honey, you just met the man!" her mother responded with concern in her voice.

I mean, after hearing only a tiny portion of my lurid past I'm sure her parents could just picture this worldly man, persuading their innocent daughter to act rashly. I could only imagine the nightmares that must have flashed through their minds at that moment of shock, and I can't fault them one bit. I had been a criminal, a dirt bag, a drug dealer, an abuser of women, an outlaw biker, and a rank reprobate. Now this innocent young woman who had no "street smarts" was agreeing to marry a man she'd only known for two weeks. But her parents hadn't met me or seen the real Jesus in me or the transforming power of Jesus Christ at work in a sinner who had once spurned God, so they couldn't know.

Sandra and I spent a lot of time together over the next few weeks as the love between us began to grow.

During that time of courtship He began to bind our hearts together with that "threefold cord that is not quickly broken." It was a time of romance and the mysterious ways of a young man and a young woman in love. But we worked at laying a sure foundation for a lasting relationship built upon the bedrock of Jesus and His Word and not the shifting sands of passion alone. We both wanted to establish a solid friendship first and control our physical intimacy until it could be sanctified in marriage.

There were a few concerned phone calls and "chance" conversations with Sandra from friends who meant well. They had heard of my background and wanted to protect Sandra from making a mistake. But we both knew in our hearts that God had brought us together.

When the time came for me to meet Sandra's parents I went to their home in fear and trembling. I wanted Sandra more than anything on earth, but I wanted her in the right way. I wanted to show her mother and father that I was a man of honor. I wasn't going to marry Sandra without her parents' blessing. I wanted to look her father in the eye and ask for his daughter's hand in marriage.

The night I met Sandra's parents their warmth and acceptance was totally disarming. They treated me with love and respect in spite of my past. They could see the sparkle in Sandra's eyes and knew that what we shared was genuine. They never sowed any seeds of doubt or rejection.

I can remember Sandra asking her mom, "Well, Mom, what do you think?"

Her mother simply said, "Honey, we trust you. You're a grown girl now, and capable of making your own decisions. We know that you know in your heart what is right. If you two are in love with each other and you feel that it is right in the eyes of God, then it's okay with your father and me."

Only six months after we met Sandra and I were married and moved into an old house in Birmingham where I became the assistant director of the Teen Challenge center for the state of Alabama. It was both a time of humble beginnings — we had tough times financially as we started out together — and of the first love of newlyweds, and God knitted us together as fellow laborers for Him as He knitted our hearts together in love.

Hired and Fired
• • •

For three years Sandra and I labored together in love to rescue young casualties from the streets of America. God brought some pretty tough cases our way, but He used them and the seasons of adversity to test us and prove us and drive home the adage that "experience is a hard teacher, because it gives the test first and the lesson afterward." Through it all He was skillfully weaving the patterns of our lives and preparing us for what lay ahead. We were nearing the third year of service at the Teen Challenge center in Birmingham when He began to stir the nest and show us that a time of change was in the wind.

About that time I received an unexpected phone call from a pastor in a church I had ministered at in Millbrook. He asked me if I would consider moving to his town and becoming the principal of the school they had in their church so I could help their young people avoid the mistakes I had learned so well. It sounded good, but I didn't want to overstep my calling and miss His will. I told him that Sandra and I would commit it to prayer and get back with him. My greatest concern was hurting Dan, who I had worked so closely with at the Teen Challenge center. For three years we had labored faithfully together, and the last thing I wanted to do was betray our friendship and trust. We had plowed like two oxen yoked together, and I didn't want to start pulling aside and miss the mark.

I went through a time of personal struggle as I agonized in prayer concerning my decision. But as much as I wrestled and pleaded with God for a clear word, "the heavens were brass and the earth iron." I finally called a close friend of mine and explained the situation. We got together for prayer. Still nothing came. After persevering in prayer for hours, Guy tapped me on the shoulder and said that he felt like he had a word from the Lord for me. He picked up his Bible and thumbed through the pages until he found the verse. "Have I not commanded you? Be strong and of good courage; do not be afraid, nor be dismayed, for the LORD your God is with you wherever you go," he read the words from the book of Joshua 1:9. "Mac, God's gonna be with you whether you go and take that job or you decide to stay at Teen Challenge."

I really felt like those words were handpicked just for me — "Fit words in due season." In two weeks Sandra and I had our car and small trailer packed with our meager belongings and were on the road for new beginnings in Millbrook, Alabama. The church provided us with a nice little house and a decent salary. We quickly settled into the comfort of our new position.

It was the calm before the storm. Twelve weeks after my hiring I was summoned to an unexpected "chat" with the pastor. The words "Ah,...Mac, can you come into my office?" triggered an immediate alarm in the back of my head. I was never good at surprise meetings in the seclusion of an office. Like I said, they always sent pangs of anxiety through me — probably flashbacks to my repeated journeys to the principal's office as a kid.

"Mac," he started in an unsteady voice, "I've been fasting and praying for four days and...I...ah," he cleared his voice. I could tell he was uncomfortable. I could sense, too, that the hammer was about to fall. "Well, the long and short of it is, Mac, I'm going to have to let you go."

I sat there glued to my seat for a long awkward moment, unable to grasp what he had just said.

"Pastor, you know that Sandra and I talked at length and really sought God in this thing, and if you remember correctly I made it very clear in the beginning that I wouldn't even consider taking this position unless you were positive God was in it. And now you're telling me that God has suddenly changed His mind?" The old Mac was rising to the surface. I was struggling hard to keep from laying hands on him suddenly, if you know what I mean.

I asked him why he had come to this conclusion. He really couldn't give me a satisfying answer, just a vague response like parents often give their children when they're up against the wall and don't really have a good reason for their decision.

All I could say was, "Well, pastor, I've been fasting the last few days also, and God hasn't told me that."

"As of right now, there's no more money comin' your way," he continued. That meant financial disaster. No money to pay the rent coming due on the big house they put us in, no money for food or utilities, and no money for gas. To top it off, we already had one child and Sandra was due with our second in just eight weeks. Even in the world outside the church if the guy you hire isn't working out you talk with him and try to work with him before you let him go. At the very least you give him a couple weeks' notice so he can find another job to put food on the table for his wife and kids.

At that moment the only thing I really wanted to do was pluck the pastor's head off his shoulders and roll it down the center aisle of the church. But something was yelling in the back of my brain that it probably wasn't the Christian thing to do.

Later that afternoon I was cleaning out my desk when he rapped on my office door and poked his head around the corner. "Can I give you a ride home?"

"No, thank you, brother," I said. "You've done enough for me. I believe I'll be okay," I said coldly.

But as I was walking down the road toward my house I began to bless the guy in spite of the injustice of it all. Little did I know at the time that God was moving behind the scenes and working this incident together for my good.

I walked through the front door of our house and Sandra looked up from the sink and said, "Hi, baby. What're you doing?"

"Oh, they just fired me from the church," I said matter-of-factly.

"You're kidding, right? Why are you home so early?" she asked.

"No, honey, I'm not kidding. I'm serious," I said.

Well, I had already learned never to underestimate the speed of gossip. Word of my unceremonious dismissal had leaked and rushed through the Christian grapevine like a wildfire. Within hours my phone was ringing off the hook by disgruntled church members in an uproar over my abrupt termination. But the Lord had already dealt with me after I had broken the news to Sandra. He told me to hold my peace and surrender the entire situation to Him.

I remember telling the first caller, "Bite your tongue, brother. I don't want you sowing any discord in the body or stirring up any strife. I don't know why the pastor did what he did. I don't know what God's doing right now, but I do know that no matter how dark or long the tunnel Jesus is holding my hand and He is going to lead us out safely."

The next morning I called a pastor friend of mine, Howard Reynolds, and explained the situation to him. I'll never forget his seasoned words of comfort and encouragement. "Well, Mac, praise the Lord! You're in the best place you could be right now. Listen, you're not bound to any church program or religious structure and you are absolutely free to get the perfect will of God for your life. For as long as I have known you, brother, the bottom line of your heart has been your desire to have His perfect will. Take courage, dear brother; there's no counsel or power or might in the world that can destroy the will of God for your life! If God's closed one door I guarantee you that He will open another one in the near future. Besides, Mac, you've spent your Christian life trusting in Him by faith. He doesn't want you fat and comfortable in a big church where you don't have to depend on Him for His provision. My bet is that He is showing you that He wants you to keep looking to Him."

His simple words of wisdom were like a cluster bomb going off in my heart. They really struck a cord.

No Gold or Glory

•••

Sandra and I were completely trusting Jesus, knowing things would be okay a few days later. We were sitting in the living room of some close friends discussing the ins and outs of where we should go from there. Dick and Donna Lovelady had grown close to us during our time with the Teen Challenge center in Birmingham. Dick was a successful businessman in the community of Birmingham and shared the same heartfelt burden for the lost youth of our country. On more than one occasion he had offered to help finance me in a youth ministry if I ever left Teen Challenge. However, it was an offer I had to refuse, because of my commitment to Dan Delcamp. I wasn't about to violate my integrity and commitments just to satisfy the urge to have my own ministry. I wasn't looking for gold or glory; I just wanted to stay in the center of His will and be obedient to what He was clearly directing me to do.

We were sitting around the coffee table when Dick said, "Mac, if you had more money than you knew what to do with...I mean, just suppose this anonymous benefactor showed up at your front door one day like that guy in "The Millionaire" and handed you a cashier's check for a million dollars. What would you do with it?" he said as he took a sip from his cup of coffee and looked over to his wife.

I remember looking at him and Donna. Big tears started flowing down my face. "I'll tell you what I would do with it. I'd buy some land and I'd start a home for young men and those who are hurting. I'd help them come out of the bondage they're in, out of Egypt, and go to a Promise Land — to Canaan Land. I'd take them and give them a home where they could find real love. Sandra and I would give them understanding and affection. They'd find the presence of God there." I looked at them for a moment and went on, "Dick, you know that Scripture in Luke 4:18 that says, Jesus came to heal the brokenhearted? I don't care what causes the broken heart, I just know that Jesus has the answers to heal it. Dick, there's hurtin' people out there by the thousands. They're dying on the streets and back alleys and our government doesn't have any answers. Jails don't have the answers. The police don't have the answers. Jesus has the answers. Dick, I would take that money and invest it in our youth by building a home so that these men could find a way out of their bondage. They would be unchained from the sin that binds them so they could feel what it is like to be really free for the first time in their lives. I'd do it with no strings attached. I wouldn't charge them one cent. I wouldn't even charge their families. It would be paid for by the Lord Jesus Christ! I would call the place 'Canaan Land Ministries!'"

We all sat silent around that coffee table for a few moments as tears flowed down my face.

Dick and Donna looked at me, and then they looked at each other. They looked at me again, then looked at Sandra holding our little Rachel on her lap. Dick stood up and said, "Mac Gober, if that don't beat all! You'd think that if somebody gave you all that money at least you'd buy yourself a nice house for your family. And the first thing you'd do with it is give it to a bunch of kids off the streets that could care less about you, that would spit in your face and cuss you out! You're telling me that you'd still turn around and help them out!"

"Dick, I've been thrown through walls. I've had spit running down my face and had kids cuss me up one side and down the other. There was a time in my life I would have ripped a man apart if he even looked at me wrong. But Jesus has given me a love and compassion for guys who are in the same place I was in not so long ago. I know Jesus hung on that cross for them, too, and if they're good enough for Jesus, they're good enough for Sandra and me."

I asked Dick and Donna if we could join hands and pray together. We stood to our feet around the coffee table.

"Dick, I don't have any money," I said before we prayed, "but I've got God. I don't own any land, either, but we've got a home we're renting now. We're going to start taking in kids off the streets as soon as we can and give them a place to stay. That's gonna be our first 'Canaan Land.' My wife is in complete agreement with me on this. We don't own anything that really belongs to us. It's all really His anyway and all that we have we are going to use to help hurting young people."

We drove back to our home that night shedding tears of joy that God had used that simple get-together to speak to our hearts. Well, that anonymous individual never did show up with a check for a million dollars, but God did use Dick in a roundabout way to clarify God's vision for our lives. We would soon learn the scriptural truth that "A man's heart plans his way, But the Lord directs his steps."

When we got back home I called up the pastor who had fired me only a couple of days before. Since we had last spoken God had given me a new perspective on the whole situation.

"Pastor, can I talk to you before we go to church tonight?" I asked him over the phone.

"Yeah, sure. Please come by," he said.

"Pastor, I want to tell the people at tonight's service that this whole thing is in God's hands. I want to tell them that you didn't know why you were letting me go but God was in it all. I also want to tell them that I still consider you to be my pastor and that this is still our home church and nothing has changed that. You may not know this, but the Lord used you to show Sandra and me that He wants us to start a Canaan Land Ministries. He just didn't want me to get comfortable in this church and tied down to a bunch of responsibilities that would have kept me from doing what He wants me to do. He doesn't want me to look to you or the people for my money. I'm not upset with you. In fact, we're thankful you did what you did. God has worked it together for our good!"

No sooner had I finished when his eyes pooled with tears and he said, "You would do this for me, Mac?"

"Brother, I love you. We're gonna win souls together!"

God supernaturally started sending young men to Sandra and me. Parents started calling us and pleading with us to help their sons. In short order our rented house was like the little old lady's shoe. We had every space in that home filled with young men. They were sleeping in the basement, in the living room, and even in our spare bedroom. You'd have to carry a flashlight at night just so you wouldn't step on anyone.

I was preaching in other churches to spread the vision and I was telling everyone, "If you don't have a home you can come and live with Sandra and me; we'll make a home for you. There's always room for one more at the cross."

I was in Texas preaching one time and I called home to Sandra, "How's it going, honey?"

"Mac, there's this guy who showed up here tonight and he's an ex-Hell's Angel. He looks real bad — real rough — and he smells terrible." I could hear the concern in her voice.

"Well, honey, all he's looking for is a little love. You just take him in and feed him. I'll be home in a couple of days."

We had already established a regular routine for the guys — Bible studies in the morning and assigned chores. Some did the cleaning, some did the cooking, and some did the dishes. I came home from my trip to Texas to find this ol' Hell's Angel sitting in the living room rocking little Rachel on his lap, tickling her under the chin, and chortling, "Gitchee-gitchee-goo!" The Spirit of God was melting old hard hearts and changing lives.

It wasn't long before we ran out of space. The men just kept coming, but we didn't know where to put them. It was about that time that I was awakened from sleep late at night by a distraught voice on the other end of the telephone.

"Hello," I said in a groggy-sounding voice as I propped myself up in my bed.

"Mr. Gober, somebody was up here preachin' in Pennsylvania and told me if I could get with you I could get some help," a man's voice was quivering on the other end.

"What they're trying to tell you is you need Jesus. I can't help you, but I can introduce you to someone who can help you. Right now we are full and have no more room here. Let me give you the phone numbers of a few places who do what we do. Maybe they can help. If you absolutely can't find any place, if something happens and you can't get into any of these places, you call me back tomorrow night," I told him.

About ten o'clock the next night the phone rang again. "Mr. Gober," I could hear the desperation in his voice.

"Yeah, this is he," I said.

"I've called all those places like you said and not a one of them can take me in. It's gonna be four months at the earliest. Mr. Gober, my veins are collapsing and I don't have four months. Please help me," he pleaded from the other end of the line.

I lowered the phone and lay there for a moment in my bed with my mind racing back to a time when I was a drugged-up motorcycle hoodlum who'd reached the bottom of the gutter. I felt empathy for the desperate stranger begging me for a helping hand. Tears began to trickle down my face as I raised the phone to my mouth. "Son, you just come on home. We'll make room for you somehow!" I assured him, and he started sobbing on the other end.

"Oh, thank you, Mr. Gober," he said.

"It's gonna be all right. Jesus is going to give you a safe trip here," I told him before I prayed and laid the receiver back to rest.

Canaan Land

• • •

The steady tide of incoming men pushed our living quarters to the limits. There was no more floor space for them to sleep on, so I started looking upward. One morning I asked the Lord, "Please help me find some bunk beds so we won't have to turn anyone away. I'm going to start stacking them two-by-two if I've got to, Lord. I can't say no to some kid who's hurting and reaching out for help, and you know that, Lord."

I started going over the classified ads and calling around to scrounge up any bunk beds that were available. But every number I dialed was a dead end. I went down the columns, crossing off the garage sales and moving ads that didn't have any beds, until I reached the bottom of the list. I called the number that advertised used bunk beds for sale.

"Yes, sir," I said when a man answered the phone. "You still got any of those bunk beds for sale you advertised?"

"I got seventy-two of 'em. How many do you want?" a man answered.

I felt like I'd just shoveled into a lost gold mine. "Whatd'ya have seventy-two bunk beds for anyway?" I asked.

"Well, me and my wife and six children live out here in Autaugaville, Alabama, on seventy acres of land and there's a lodge on the property that'll sleep seventy-two people if you put four men to a room." My mind was reeling as he described the place. "And then there's an A-frame chapel, too. It's a beautiful place with rolling hills and a creek that runs through the property. It used to have a dam, but it broke a few years back, and the lake is empty now. But it shouldn't be too much trouble putting it back to make a twenty-five-acre lake," he finished.

All I could think about when he was describing his property was what a perfect place it would be for a bunch of kids who needed help. My mind was in a dream zone as I tried to visualize it.

"Sir, is your place for sale?" I asked.

"Well it's negotiable," he answered.

"Whatd'ya mean?" I countered.

"Well, last year I had it listed in the paper for $285,000. It's not even up for sale right now. It's not in the paper, and I don't have it listed with a realtor. It's just sitting out here. To be honest with you, things have been kinda hard for us lately, and I'm selling the bunk beds just to put some food on the table for my family."

"I'll be there in an hour to look at the place, if you don't mind," I said.

I was so excited I called a close friend of mine, Dr. Robert Parker, who was a veterinarian on my board. His receptionist said he was operating on a dog but if

I'd hold she'd try and see if he could talk with me for a moment.

"Mac, what can I do for you? I'm in surgery now so I'll have to make this quick," Dr. Parker answered the phone shortly after.

"Robert, you won't believe what just happened. I found this property and it's perfect. I mean, I could put all the men in there and there's room to grow and there's seventy acres with a chapel." I was pouring out the words so fast in my excitement that Dr. Parker had to cut me off.

"Mac, whoa, slow down, slow down," he said, "I can't stop operating on this dog. I'm right in the middle of the operation."

"Well, I've got to go over and see this place for myself," I responded.

"Okay, Mac, go over and check it out and then give me and the rest of the board a report," he said.

I drove over to the property feeling like a six-year-old on his first trip to Disneyland. As soon as I stepped out of the car I knew that I had found Canaan Land. I looked around at all the towering pine trees, the rolling hills of green grass, and the spreading oaks, and I knew in my heart this was the place. It was terribly run-down and grown over from years of neglect, but I had a vision of what the place could be with a lot of hard work and loving care.

The owner walked down the driveway and shook my hand. We walked around the property together until we reached the top of the hill.

"Would you consider selling this place to me?" I looked him in the eyes and asked.

"Well, Mac...I don't know. Maybe for the right price I would consider it," he answered.

"Well, I'm gonna bring my board out here to look it over and I'll make you an offer," I said.

That night I went to work and called all the board members. They all agreed to go back with me to survey the property. The next day we pulled up in Dick Lovelady's custom van. I introduced my board members to the owner, who then proceeded to show us around. Some of my board members excelled in business and were walking around with a pocket calculator adding things up as we went. When we got back to the van I asked the owner if we could have a few minutes to ourselves.

"Well, what's the verdict guys?" I asked eagerly.

"Mac, don't offer him a penny more than $150,000," Larry Blasingame said firmly.

"But can't I offer him $250 thou or something more reasonable?" I said.

"Listen, Mac, this place has seen better days and is in pretty bad shape. It's worth only $150,000 on a fair market value with all these buildings sitting on this land out here in the middle of nowhere," Dick said and the others nodded in agreement.

Larry and I walked back up the hill to present our offer to the owner.

"Well, did you come up with anything?" he said.

"Yes, sir, we would like to offer you $150,000 for the whole thing," I said.

The guy did a double take, choked, and cleared his throat. "Mr. Gober, I can't give the place away," he said in a bewildered-sounding voice. "I won't sell it to you at that price!"

"Now, look," I got bold. The presence of God came upon me. I looked him squarely in the face and said, "Sir, $150,000 is more than a fair offer. If you sell this place you'll sell it to me and you'll sell it for $150,000. We're getting in that van down there and we're going home in a couple of minutes. When you get ready to sell it to us you let me know," I finished as I turned to leave.

We drove home. Larry and his wife spent the night at my house before heading home to Mississippi the next day. As they were leaving the next morning his wife said she would like to see the property for herself, so Larry said he'd take her up there before they went home.

They drove up to the place and looked around without getting out of the car. They were turning around to leave when the owner came running down the drive, hollering and tapping the windshield of their car. Larry rolled down the window. The guy was breathing hard and panting. "If you guys'll put your offer down in writing I'll sell this place to Mac Gober for $150,000," he said.

Instead of going straight home Larry and his wife turned around and headed back to my house. I remember seeing them pulling up in the driveway and thinking to myself that they must have forgotten something. Larry climbed out of the car with this big grin on his face like he'd swallowed the Cheshire cat.

"Mac," he smiled, "Congratulations! You just bought yourself seventy acres for $150,000!"

I started jumping up and down and shouting and praising the Lord. I was beside myself with joy, but I didn't know what I was all excited about. I didn't even have two nickels in my pocket to rub together. I knew that it would take a lot more than that to fix up the place.

Out of Africa

• • •

Within a few days the legal papers were drawn up and the contract for Canaan Land signed. It was a done deal in writing, but I was facing the challenge of raising the money to pay for it.

The paperwork was completed in December. At that time I was facing additional pressure of raising money to participate in a large crusade in Africa, which I had previously committed to. A team of twenty-one people, including myself, from all over the U.S. were set to minister in crusades in Kenya. But with the signing of the papers for Canaan Land the financial burden of traveling to Africa seemed like an impossibility.

I prayed and said, "Lord, I want to go, but I don't have the money. Feeding these men right now is about all that I can handle. It's gonna take You to open the windows of heaven and pour out a blessing. If You want me to go I'll go, but You've got to provide a way."

I remember just finishing that prayer and sitting down on my couch when the phone rang. It was a man calling from Texas.

"Mac, the Lord just spoke to me and told me to give you a call and ask you what your need was."

Now, I hadn't seen this man for over two years and all of a sudden he calls out of the blue.

"Well, sir," I said, "the Lord's been dealin' with my heart to go to Africa and minister in this major crusade. I'm one of the main speakers and we expect crowds of thirty-five to forty thousand people each night. The truth is, I don't have the money to go. When you called I had just finished asking the Lord to provide the money if He wanted me to go."

"Mac, you just tell me how much it's gonna cost. I'll write you out a check right this minute and drop it in the mail," he said without a moment of hesitation.

That unexpected blessing was met with a severe attack from the enemy when I was in Kenya. We had been ministering for several days when I woke up from a fitful sleep about four o'clock one morning with the devil taunting me, "Who do you think you are? You go out and foolishly spend $150,000 you don't have on some stupid piece of property that needs $50,000 maintenance. Now you've got the gall to ask God to pay for it? Here you are all the way over in Africa doing your own thing. You've left Sandra and all those guys you're suppose to be helping back home without money to pay for that property!"

I bolted upright in my bed and tried to shake the nagging thoughts from my mind. I knew it was the enemy attacking me. I started rebuking the devil out loud in the hut we were sleeping in. "I'll tell you who I am!" I shot back. "I'm a son of God and the servant of Jesus Christ. Let me tell you something, Devil, you're nothin' but 'The Accuser of the Brethren,' just like the Bible says. You never stop trying to destroy what God is doing in the earth. It's not my idea to build this home for young men, but God's. God's going to provide for it whether you like it or not! And if God wants to build it you ain't going to stop it. I'm not in this for fame or money or to build myself some little kingdom. I just want to help these hurting young men find Jesus."

By that time the Holy Ghost had come upon me. I'd started preaching out loud so that I woke up my fellow preachers and attracted a crowd of Kenyans who started filling up the hut. They were pressing into it with their blankets wrapped around them. For two hours I preached under the anointing of the Holy Ghost. When I finished men and women were weeping and praising God all through the place.

Ray Ables, a pastor from Louisiana, came up to me and said, "Brother Mac, you have blessed our lives this day. You have ministered to our wives and our children. God was truly in this place. Brother Mac, is there some need that you have that we can pray for?"

"Yes, sir," I said point blank. "I need $200,000 to buy a home for boys! I need for God to move in a powerful way!" I didn't expect the heavens to part and $200,000 to fall out of the sky or for one of those poor Africans to pull out a check, but I felt an unction to proclaim the need so everyone could hear.

A spontaneous sound of prayer and praise shook the hut as people began to cry out to God to make a way where there seemed to be none. The chorus continued for several minutes before it began to die down. A solemn hush fell upon those who were gathered. Just then one of the pastors who was sitting on a bed next to me began to speak out the Word of the Lord. "Mac, God's gonna give you that land!" he said with conviction in his voice as he cupped his face in his hands and began to cry. "He's gonna raise up eight hundred Christians to give a onetime love gift of $250. They're going to stand with you, Mac, and be your partners."

"Brother Mac, I want to be the first to stand with you," another pastor shouted.

"Hey! I want in on this too!" I shouted. "You guys aren't gonna leave me and Sandra out of this blessing!" I laughed.

Within a matter of minutes several thousand dollars in pledges came from that small group of men. When we returned to the States eighteen of the twenty-one people on that team went out and spread the word that I couldn't say no to that young man in Pennsylvania who had called late one night in desperation and I wasn't going to say no to anyone else who needed our help. Over the next couple of years all eight hundred pledges came in, because of the faithfulness of men and women across America who share Sandra's and my burden for the lost and wounded youth of our country.

In time we raised a huge thirty-three-foot cross on the spot where the previous owner had said he wouldn't sell the property to me for the price I offered. It's a large white cross with the name of Jesus written in gold letters across it and floodlights at its base to light it up at night as a reminder of the abiding love and faithfulness of our Savior.

Through a lot of hard work, blisters, sweat, and prayer, we turned that run-down retreat into a refuge for young men. We planted a beautiful garden around that cross with a water fountain and flowers. It's a prayer garden where the men can carry their troubles and seek the presence of God in prayer at the foot of the cross.

The Lord also impressed upon me to construct a large Bible out of concrete and engrave the names of all eight hundred pledge partners who had helped make Canaan Land possible. I know that there are some who would criticize this, but I didn't do it for the praise of man. I didn't do it because those who sacrificed needed some kind of earthly recognition. I did it for the men who have found their way to Canaan Land. So many times over the years one of them has walked by that big Bible lying open with those names engraved in brass and said to me, "Brother Mac, nobody out there really cares about me," and I have pointed to those names and told him, "See those names. They care. They may never step onto this land, but there are hundreds of men and women out there who care about you!" There has been many times over the years when one of those young men has walked across the property at night feeling broken and discouraged. He has looked at the Bible and glanced up to the cross all lit up and has known that there are a lot of people out there pulling and praying for him, and it has been just enough encouragement to keep him going.

Over the years God has given Canaan Land great favor. We haven't had the money to pay for advertisements or television ads, but the Lord has provided the way to tell men and women all across America of a place where troubled youth can find deliverance. He's repeatedly opened doors through the 700 Club and radio and talk shows. The attorney general of Alabama officially has endorsed our ministry to judges and the courts and even supports us out of his own pocket. He has stood behind us with the weight of his office and publicly declared that Canaan Land is a public asset. He has told the citizens of our state that this ex-outlaw biker has a reputation for impeccable character with the law enforcement agencies of the state — so much for an old motorcycle hoodlum who God saved from the world.

Growing strongly from its humble beginnings, Canaan Land has impacted the lives of thousands across this country over the years. It has grown into several more Canaan Lands — in the Caribbean, Canada, and Africa — as a result of its success in turning young people around.

C H A P T E R 2 2

Tribe of Judah
Motorcycle Ministry
• • •

Ten years had passed since I had climbed off of my
old Harley. My motorcycle days were a painful part of
my past — a past I had tried to bury. The whole lifestyle
had been such a seductive force in my life. It took ten
years before I finally felt a release to ride again.

In the mid-eighties the Lord began to speak to me
about taking Jesus back to the streets. In short order God
began to use a Harley and my past experiences to reach a
multitude of hurting souls, lost on the asphalt arteries of
America. It didn't happen overnight, but the Lord began
to lead my steps back to those I had left behind. And even
though I got some flak from a few — who said I shouldn't
go back to the streets on a Harley Davidson to share the
gospel that way — there are hundreds of saved men and
women today who are glad I listened to God.

I was ministering in New York City on the streets
with Pastor Paul Costa, who used to be a tight end for
the Buffalo Bills. Paul asked me if I would mind doing
him a favor by visiting a friend of his in New York State
Prison. He pulled some strings and got permission from
the authorities for me to go behind the bars to talk with

some of the inmates. While there, I went to see Larry L. At that time he was president of "The Tribe," an outlaw motorcycle club that was later consumed by another club out west. Larry was doing hard time for various crimes. I had heard of Larry's reputation and wanted to share my testimony with him.

I remember being escorted down a series of corridors by a couple of stern-looking prison guards. One of them asked me, "Man, you sure you want in there with this man all by yourself? Are you sure you know who you're fixin' to talk to? Take it from me, this guy is nothin' but an animal!"

"Hey, I hear ya, officer. That's what they used to say about me," I replied. "If you'll just let us have a room by ourselves and leave us alone for a while everything will be okay."

They shook their heads and said, "Have it your way, man, but we still think you may be making a big mistake."

I remember the sound of the guards' shoes tapping on the linoleum floor as we marched down the last corridor to a large prison door. One of the guards instructed another to open the door and the massive steel gate rolled open. We stepped through. I could hear the clicking and rumbling of the door as it slid shut and slammed into place behind us. We walked down another hallway to another door with a guard standing outside.

"Hey, Norton," one of my escorts said to the guard standing outside the door. "This is Mac Gober. He's here to see Larry L."

The guard turned and opened the door with a set of keys. "You gotta visitor, Larry," the guard said. "He's all yours," my escort said as he motioned me into the room. It was all white with a small metal table and two chairs. Larry was sitting in one of them staring intensely at the opposite wall. "We'll be down the hall if you need us," the guard added.

I walked into the barren room, looked at Larry, and said, "Hi, Larry, my name is Mac Gober." At first he just sat there defiantly with a stone-cold look on his face. I could tell by the lines in his face that he had done a lot of hard road miles on the outside. At first he didn't want anything to do with me. He probably thought I was some goodie-two-shoes preacher come to rattle his cage. But after a few moments of sharing some of my own past he began to warm up a bit. He could tell from the language I used and the things I told him that I wasn't some phony who didn't know what he was talking about. I'd walked in his shoes and knew what it was like to ride with a club. We talked shop for a few minutes and compared notes of the places we'd been and the things we had done.

"Brother," Larry cut me off. "You're like no preacher I've ever run into. I mean, you come all the way in here to talk with me and you're not stickin' your hand in my pocket to get some money or askin' for somethin' in return. And you sure ain't no narc or pig. And look at you, man; I've never seen a preacher wearin' jeans and open shirt and cowboy boots," he said in surprise as I smiled back. "But I'll tell you one thing, Mac. I can tell you're sincere. You sound like what you're saying is comin' from the heart."

"I do care, Larry," I said sincerely, "and I want you to know that Jesus cares about you too, brother. He didn't just come down to some prison. He came down to an entire world bound in sin and gave His very life on the cross to deliver each of us from the chains of sin and spiritual bondage. He did it for me, Larry, and He wants to do it for you. That's why I came down here, just to talk with you face to face. I wanted to tell you that I love you and Jesus loves you and there is a way out of this prison, but it starts deep down in your heart.

"Larry, I've gotta go soon, but I want to know if you'll get down on your knees and pray with me. I'm not going to con you, man, or try and force you. You're a man. It takes a real man with courage to reach out to Jesus and admit that you're a sinner and you need for Him to be your Savior. I'm not gonna embarrass you, Larry. I'm just tellin' you like it is. Jesus is the way and He's got more power than all the armies of the world and all the firepower of all the motorcycle clubs in the world. He'll use His power to set you free and help you if you'll just ask Him."

Tears were filling Larry's eyes as he looked at me and nodded. The Holy Spirit came upon both of us so strong. We knelt for a few moments and prayed.

"Time's up!" One of the jailers rapped on the outside of the door.

"I love ya, man," I said as I gave Larry a big hug and shook his hand. "Thanks for letting me talk with you, brother. Just remember that Jesus loves you no matter what. Keep your eyes on Him and He'll do the rest."

In the mid-80s my path crossed with another ex-outlaw biker who had been raised by an outlaw club. After meeting Ben Priest and his wife, Tammy, I found out that God had put two jewels, two cameos in a dark world where a lot of the church people would never go. God had raised up Ben and Tammy to take the love of Jesus into the world of outlaw bikers uncompromisingly, just because they cared. I have never seen such boldness and such honesty in a ministry in all my life.

I remember Ben sharing with me one time his life's personal story. No television cameras were around, no radio mikes, no newspaper reporters, just Ben sitting there sharing with me. As he began to share his story, I began to cry. I mean tears flooded my face. I realized he had been through the years of hurt and pain that I had been through and then some. Ben told me about when he was born again and the experience he had. What a miracle story of how God saved Ben Priest. The love of God is so big in his heart that he and his wife could do nothing else, I feel, except for what God had called them to do. It was a supernatural act of God.

Ben went to Bible school and did everything that he knew to be obedient to God, but he just felt like he didn't fit in where everyone else fit in. He couldn't play the piano, he couldn't sing, he couldn't do a lot of the things other people did in the ministry. He said, "God all I know to do is ride scooters, and I don't even have a scooter. If you will give me a scooter, I will take the love of Jesus back into the outlaw world."

Supernaturally, the next day, a lady came up and said, "Hey, you know my husband died several years ago and there is an old motorcycle out in the garage. I feel like the Lord wants me to give it to you, and I don't really know if you would want it or not."

Ben walked out of there thinking he didn't have any money to buy this motorcycle, not knowing that God was giving it to him. It just happened to be a 1950 panhead. Are you kidding me! Is God good or what!

He got that old thing out and cleaned it up, and worked on it for a while. As he fired her up and was heading down the highway one day — as he was cruising down there on that old hard tail on the country roads of Mississippi — he said it felt like the fire of God came out of heaven and burned a patch into his back. It said *Tribe of Judah* with a big gold cross and Jesus is Lord on the bottom of it.

As he was riding out there early on a Sunday morning, an outlaw club was on the side of the road taking a break. Ben pulled in there and started talking to one of the men. Another old boy quickly pulled out a gun and had it up in Ben's face threatening to shoot him. Ben was not afraid or intimidated. He just began to tell them you can't kill a dead man, and that he had already died with Christ, and that he was there to tell them about the Lord. The president of the club told everybody to be quiet and shut up. Come to find out the president of that club, while he was in prison, had made a promise to God that when he got out he was going to serve God, but he failed to do it. He felt like God had sent Ben that early Sunday morning to him. It was not an accident. It was a divine appointment for that biker, and to show Ben Priest what his calling in life would really be.

Then Ben got down on his knees and prayed with all those bikers. At the president's request, they all got down on their knees and prayed. Ben led them all to the Lord Jesus Christ, and then invited them to go to church with him. Since he was just out taking a good morning putt, they all got on their scooters and followed Ben back to church. That was the beginning of the Tribe of Judah.

Today, there are a lot of men and women who will be in heaven because of the love of Jesus Christ through the Tribe of Judah ministry — men and women who were lost and on their way to hell. It has touched their lives and literally thousands around the world today. Thank God for men and women like Ben and Tammy Priest, who have received the call of God on their lives to take the love of Jesus to the streets and to the hard places. I count it a great honor and privilege to have some small part in riding in the Tribe of Judah, to be with some of the greatest men and women of God on this earth.

If you want to know anything about the Tribe of Judah motorcycle ministry, then I urge you to contact Ben and Tammy Priest at P.O. Box 2423, Humble, Texas 77347.

Over the years I have had my share of burley bikers stick their middle finger in my face and tell me to "take Jesus and shove it!" But I have also seen my share of men and women who have turned their lives over to Christ. As tough and mean as some of those bikers could be, there was usually a heart of gold under the layers of road time and hardness of the biker lifestyle. More often than not, beneath all the trappings of the biker mystique are hurting hearts of men and women who simply long for love and understanding and, most of all, the truth. Many tolerated us, if not openly accepted us, because we weren't there to lay some heavy religious trip on them, preach down to them, or condemn their lifestyle. We'd climbed back on our scoots so we could "become all things to all men" in the hopes that we might "save some." We'd become like them so we could show them that we care — to show them that we had not come to spy on them, dig up dirt for the police, or bring any heat down on their heads. We simply wanted to reach out with a helping, listening ear, and a simple message of God's love for His people.

We have often had to plow long and till the soil with a delicate hand, but God has given us favor and opened doors to hearts and minds that no man can shut. There have been times when we've been invited into outlaw biker clubhouses to talk with the members. They've invited us in because they have tried us and seen that we aren't phonies. And in the midst of those places filled with weapons God has come down with the power of the Holy Ghost and touched the stoniest of hearts.

On one of our outreaches at the famous Sturgis biker rally, Ben and I were ministering on the main street of Sturgis at 2:00 a.m. to this guy from Sturgis who had lost one of his arms in a motorcycle accident. Several hundred thousand bikers and groupies had converged on the town for the annual gathering and had packed the surrounding campgrounds and hillsides with bikers of all persuasions.

Ben was kneeling next to the guy by the curb, talking to him about his need for Jesus, when I walked up just after I'd led a brother biker to the Lord.

"What's holding you back from surrendering your life to Him?" Ben asked.

"'Cause if I do it right here on the street my wife would never believe I did it for real," he said.

"Then why don't you do it right in front of your wife and kids?" I responded.

"But she's at home with the kids," he answered.

"Look, man, you're down here by yourself partying and blowin' your mind and you know in your heart that your wife and kids love you and want you back, right?" I exhorted him. "If that's the case, Ben and I will go back with you and we'll pray with you right in the presence of your wife."

The guy looked up at us with a shocked expression on his face. "You...You would really do that for me?" he asked. "It's two in the morning!"

"Man, that's why we're here!" I told him.

When we got to his house that night his wife was standing in front of the sink looking outside as three bikers walked up the front steps. When we stepped inside she had a worried look on her face, like she was thinking to herself, "Oh, Lord, what now?" But as Ben turned to shut the door I could see her looking at the patch on the back of his rag, which read, "The Tribe of Judah Motorcycle Ministry — Jesus is Lord!" She started crying that her prayers had been answered. We found out she was a Christian woman who had been praying for her husband to get saved.

We told her what happened and her husband looked at her and said that he wanted her to see that it was for real as he knelt down on his hands and knees and asked Jesus into his heart. We were all kneeling there on the floor crying and thanking Jesus. We walked out of that house that night under an inky black sky strewn with a thousand stars — like they were saying how wonderful it was that somebody cared enough to leave the four walls of a church to go out into the world to where the lost are living and tell them the good news of salvation.

Over the years I have had the privilege of being on the 700 Club many times to share my testimony. Hearing my testimony, men from my past have called the phone banks to ask for prayer. Without giving their names they have asked the listener to please tell Mac they used to run with me out in California. I've had the privilege of praying with some of the most notorious bikers and telling them that our God is not a respecter of persons but a loving God who loves them.

Only a short time ago one of our staff paged me to tell me I had a long-distance phone call. I picked up the receiver and heard a raspy voice on the other end say, "Hello, Mac, this is Larry."

My mind went racing back over all the years trying to remember the name, but I drew a complete blank. I have talked to so many people all over the world over the years that many a name gets lost in my memory.

"It's me, Larry...The guy eight years ago in the New York State Prison you prayed for. Remember, I gave you a hard time at first until I realized that you were for real?" he said as the tumblers began to line up in my head. "That day that you prayed with me in my cell was the first time any man had ever prayed with me or even offered me a chance to pray. And that day Jesus Christ came into my life!"

"Yeah, Larry...I do remember now, brother," I said.

"Well, Mac, after that happened God began to work in my heart and I could tell that He was changing me. I mean, something wonderful came over me, and all of a sudden I realized for the first time in my life that I had hope — that God was alive and He cared for me. I got a Bible and started reading it and began attending a prayer group in the joint. When I got out God restored my marriage and my family and now I travel all over the country, telling people about what God has done for me," he said as his voice broke up and he started crying. I started crying with him. "And, Brother Mac, I just wanted to tell you what that day meant and to tell you never to be discouraged about sharing your testimony with guys like me. No matter what church I share at I always tell 'em about this man named Mac Gober who God sent into my cell — an old ex-knothead, ex-motorcycle hoodlum, who understood where I lived and didn't put me down, but just told me about the love of Jesus...And, Mac, I just thought you needed to know."

Legacy
• • •

I never had the opportunity to see my grandfather alive after I got saved. The last memories I have of him are seeing his body lying paralyzed on that old feather bed. He died in his sleep when I was still running drugs with my biker buddies out west.

Two years after I received Jesus my grandmother asked me to come and visit her in that old farmhouse I had known so well in my youth. She told me that pastor John Young of Jasper, Alabama, wanted me to come share my testimony in his church in Nauvoo, Alabama. She also said that she had something important she needed to tell me — something she had kept in the secrecy of her heart for many years.

It was a crisp, cold day in the dead of winter when I stepped into that old drafty farm house I had enjoyed so much in my childhood. It was one of those cold lifeless days when it seemed like all the colors of the countryside had turned to toneless grays — one of those forlorn days that seemed so quiet and forsaken.

When I walked through the door of my grandmother's house she grabbed me by her weathered hands and just hugged me with her face buried in my chest — that little frail woman hugging the prodigal grandson who had finally come home. She stood there hugging me and telling me how proud she was that I was now following Jesus. After a few moments of embrace she took my hand and led me through that little shack of a house with that same old potbelly stove fighting back the cold to the one bedroom just off the front room. Still standing where it had for years was that old feather bed I had slept on under mountains of quilted blankets as a child — the same bed my grand-daddy had spent the last years of his life in.

We stood there before the bed like we were paying silent respect at a grave side. It was empty now — resting empty of the man who had meant so much to me. I stood there looking down on the place where he had occupied the twilight years of his life, aching in my heart that I had not been able to tell him how sorry I was — not able to kiss him on the cheek and say goodbye until we could meet on the other side.

"You know, son, your granddaddy loved you so," my grandmother said as she gently squeezed my hand.

"Yes ma'am, I know that," I said with a lump in my throat. The emotions began to well up from deep within my soul. Bittersweet memories flooded my mind — remorseful memories of standing in the same spot at the end of that old brass bed in my grubby biker garb and shaggy head of hair thinking how bad I was, thinking how I knew what was happening. They were painful, stabbing memories of another Mac Gober standing there in my pride and self-conceit thinking to myself that I had beat the odds because I was so tough, oblivious to the fact that it was God all along who had spared my miserable life out of His great love and mercy when I deserved to go to hell. It was another arrogant grandson who had stood at the foot of that bed looking down at a crippled wisp of a man and thinking to himself, "You poor old dirt farmer." And I choked back the sorrow and remorse.

"You know, son, your granddaddy loved you so," she said again, as if her own thoughts had also drifted back to the same reflections.

"Yes, ma'am," I confessed.

"I don't know if you know this, but do you realize that you're the only Gober left now in our family? And if you had died in Vietnam there'd be no more Gobers to carry on our family name? If you had died in your sins out there in California there would be no one left to carry on the heritage," she said.

"Yes, ma'am," I replied quietly.

"But what you don't know, son, and I've held this in my heart for many years until you were ready to hear it, is this." She turned to look at me with eyes watering with tears. "Every Sunday the men folk would come out to the house after church and they'd drive out to our home and sit and visit a spell with your granddaddy and me. And many a time your granddaddy would ask the men folk to lift him out of this bed and place his body in a praying position, bent down on his knees beside the bed. And when they would fold his hands together," she said, wiping tears from her eyes, "they would hold on to him and prop him up beside the bed and he would lean over it with his hands closed together in prayer and cry out to God to save his grandson who was lost in sin in California."

As I stood there stunned, listening to what she was saying, it was like each word was a bomb going off in my heart. Waves of emotions washed over me with a force that was almost physical in its impact. They were simple, heartfelt words from the lips of an uneducated woman, but those simple words were more moving and eloquent to me than those of any great poet. I stood there, rain tapping impatiently on the roof, my thoughts racing back all those years to a time when I was so full of pride and so filled with myself — realizing afresh that I could have died at any moment with a bullet in the back of my head like a lot of my buddies and been dumped in some shallow grave out in the desert.

"Son, all the time you was in Vietnam and your granddaddy would be watching the news every night and they'd be a talking about Da Nang being overrun and the rockets hitting where you were at and your granddaddy would call out to God to save his grandson and keep you whole so that you could preach the gospel," she added.

I was stunned by the impact of those words and the crush of emotion that overwhelmed me.

"Your granddaddy went to be with the Lord callin' out your name, that you'd be saved one day, son. Your granddaddy wasn't alive to see it, but he knows that you're saved today," she told me.

Hearing those words and seeing the tears of joy streaming down my grandmother's face, I couldn't hold back the emotions any longer. The dam burst and I started to cry uncontrollably — deep wrenching sobs. At that moment of revelation I realized that my granddaddy was a real man of faith and courage and conviction. He wasn't a stupid old dirt farmer, but a man of faithfulness, a hardworking man, an honest man, a man who served God in faith. And at that moment I wanted to be like that poor old dirt farmer more than any man on earth.

A couple of years later my grandmother suffered a stroke that left her paralyzed on the left side of her body. She still had partial movement on the right side of her body, but could only slur her words. I remember walking into her hospital room and seeing her lying beneath the sheets, ashen, contorted, and unable to talk. She beckoned me over to her bedside with her good hand and motioned for me to turn my palm upward. As a youngster she had taught me some of the sign language she used to communicate with the deaf children who would come to the summer camp. As I sat there looking at my aged grandmother she began to hand sign these words to me.

"Son," she scribed the letters slowly, "did you know that there has always been a preacher in the Gober family? Your great-granddaddy's name was H. M. Gober (Howard Macpherson) and, son, your name is H. M. Gober also. The first H. M. was a circuit-riding preacher who traveled by horseback from town to town preaching the gospel...And your great-great-grandfather was also a preacher. He prayed that his children's children's children would serve God. Son, that's why that old devil did everything in his power to destroy you all those years. He knew that the call of God was on your life. I've got an old book I want you to have. It has been passed down through the family for many years and I want you to have it now, son." She instructed me where to find the book in a back storage room.

I went to retrieve it and found it buried in an old musty trunk. It was tattered and thumb worn from many years of use. I opened it slowly and found an old yellowed photo inside of my great-granddaddy holding a Bible. The treasure was tucked between the pages along with a little, weathered salvation tract that my great-granddaddy had written to win sinners to Christ.

I remember so profoundly the emotional impact of standing there holding those precious little reminders of a legacy that had endured the press of many years. I was so overwhelmed by the emotions that I was speechless. I stood there paralyzed by the torrent of feelings, reflecting on the heritage I had come from with hot tears coursing down cheeks swollen with emotion.

I remember so clearly how filled with gratitude and joy I was at the revelation of God's great faithfulness that answered the prayers of my grandfathers — overcome with gratefulness that He had reached down and freed me from the chains of sin and darkness that bound me for so many years.

I stepped out into the falling rain of that winter night and walked down that muddy road oblivious to the wet and cold falling around me — filled with praise and thanksgiving that God had heard the persevering prayers of my ancestors and delivered a sinner like me.

White Cross

Criminal record, drug abuse
Beating up everyone, don't wanna make a truce
Taking on dad, just to prove his point
Dropping acid and rolling a joint

A Harley Davidson and a tattoo
He's the king of this wonder world, yeah it's true
Everyone knows when he's in town
'Cause the folks at the bar start cowering down

Cops on his tail cause he's dealing drugs
And he's beating-up all of those so called "thugs"
All of this started in a war called Vietnam
Where his mind got screwed up from the war zone and the bombs

But then light kicked on and he got sense in his head
He prayed the simple prayer as he laid on the bed
His "brothers" weren't a part of his family anymore
'Cause Jesus came over and knocked on his door

He decided to leave behind the maniac
He walked away from the hog and never came back
He started his life all over again
And left behind the life of sin

Ministry to young men what's on his heart
Canaan Land was just the start
He doesn't want any gold or glory
He just wants to tell people his story

Normally it's "X" marks the spot
Instead, this time it's a white cross
At this white cross tears have been shed
Because finally a new life can be led

Canaan Land is his heart and soul
The white cross shows his life's goal
His testimony is "Unchained"
And Jesus Christ is the One you can blame

Written by Jessica Burke
Age 14, 1996

Glossary

Afternoon Putt — motorcycle expression for taking a casual afternoon ride on your bike

AK-47 — a Soviet assault rifle

ARVN — abbreviation for "Army Republic of Vietnam"

B-52 — a long-range heavy bomber

Beaucoup — French for "many"

Betel nut — an opiate chewed by some Vietnamese. It stains the user's lips red and teeth black

Beezers — slang expression for BSA motorcycles

Body bag — a plastic zipper bag for corpses

Brass — military slang for "officers"

Bronze Star — our nation's fourth highest medal

Buddy System — a program whereby friends can enlist together

Bush — the outer field areas where soldiers operated

Busted — slang expression for getting arrested for illegal drugs

Center-punch — an affectionate greeting between outlaw bikers involving a punch to the chest

Chopper — motorcycles that are stripped down to the hard frame

Citizen — biker term for ordinary civilians

Cordite — explosive compound in bombs and shells

Crank (speed) — slang expressions for methamphetamine

Cranking over — term for starting your motorcycle

C-rats, C's, — C-rations or prepackaged military meals to be eaten in the field

C-4 — high explosive putty-like material

C-130 — a cargo plane used to transport men and supplies

C-141 — a large military transport jet

Charles, Charlie, Mr. Charles, Victor Charlie — slang expression for the Viet Cong

Chieu Hoi — "open arms" or expression of surrender

Claymore — mines rigged to spray hundreds of steel pellets

Concertina Wire — barbed wire that is rolled out along the ground to hinder the progress of troops

Cycalos — pedicabs

Deuce-and-a-half — two-and-a-half-ton truck

Dung Lai — Vietnamese for "Don't Move!"

Dustoff — medical evacuation flight

EM club — abbreviation for "Enlisted Men's" club

Firebase —bases established to provide artillery support for ground units operating in the bush

Fire-mission — artillery support that has been requested

Firing off — motorcycle term for turning your engine over

Fix (fixin') — slang expression for injecting drugs intravenously

Flak jacket — a protective vest worn to protect the chest area from shrapnel and bullets

Frags — slang expression for fragmentation grenades

Fragged — slang expression for killing someone with a fragmentation grenade

Freedom Bird — slang expression for the flight that took you home after your tour was up

Friendlies — friendly Vietnamese

Gooks, Gooners, Dinks, Slopes, Zipper-heads — derogatory slang for Vietnamese

Greased — slang expression for "killed"

Grunt — slang expression for any combat soldier

Gunship — a Huey helicopter armed with machine-guns and rockets

Huey — UH-1 helicopter. Used extensively in Vietnam to transport men and supplies

Ho Chi Minh Sandals — crude sandals made from rubber tires

Hooch — slang expression for any form of dwelling place

Humping — slang expression for marching with a heavy load through the bush

IV — intravenous injection

Jap scrap/rice burners — sarcastic motorcycle term for Japanese made motorcycles

Klick — short for kilometer (1 kilometer=1,000 meters)

LZ — abbreviation for Landing Zone

Mainlining — slang expression for injecting drugs into your veins

Mama Sanh — term for an elderly Vietnamese woman

Medevac — a helicopter extraction of sick, wounded, or dead from the battlefield

Monkey Mountain — a famous mountain near Da Nang inhabited by Rock Apes

M-14 — an automatic rifle used early in the war

M-16 — a standard automatic weapon used by American and allied ground forces

M-60 — a machine gun

National Run — a motorcycle term for a large gathering of bikers

NLF — abbreviation for National Liberation Front, the political designation for the Viet Cong

Nouc-mam — a strong smelling, fermented Vietnamese fish sauce

Number One — very good

Number Ten — very bad

NVA — abbreviation for North Vietnamese Army

Panhead — slang expression for Harley Davidson motorcycles produced from 1948 to 1965

Pedicab — three-wheeled bicycle used as a taxi

Papa Sanh — a term for an elderly Vietnamese man

PCP/Angel Dust — street term for a potent drug

Point, Pointman — the lead man in a column or patrol

POL Depot — abbreviation for Petroleum, Oil, and Lubricant Depot

Popped — slang expression for getting arrested

Punji Stakes — sharpened bamboo stakes usually dipped in excrement and usually placed in pits

Rackin' pipes — motorcycle expression for revving up the throttle of your bike

Rag — slang expression for "jacket"

ROKs — Republic of Korea Marines

Roody-poot — a motorcycle term for a part-time, weekend biker who doesn't wear a patch

Sappers — enemy infiltrators whose job was to detonate explosive charges within our positions

Satchel Charges — explosive packs carried by sappers

Scoots — slang expression for a motorcycle

Scuttlebutt — Marine Corps or Navy term for "rumors"

Short-timer — someone whose tour in Vietnam was almost completed

Shovelhead — slang expression for Harley Davidson motorcycles produced from 1965 to 1984

Slick — slang expression for a Huey

Sleeves — heavily tattooed arms

Smack — slang expression for heroin

Squids — slang expression for anyone in the Navy

Tracer — a bullet with a phosphorous coating designed to burn and give a visual indication of its trajectory

Triage — the process of sorting out patients according to the seriousness of their wounds

Trumpets — motorcycle term for Triumph motorcycles

VC, Viet Cong — South Vietnamese Communists

Wannabe — a derogatory expression for someone who wants to be a real biker

Web-gear — canvas suspenders and belt used to carry an infantryman's gear

Prayer for Salvation
and Baptism in the Holy Spirit

Heavenly Father, I come to You in the Name of Jesus. Your Word says, "Whosoever shall call on the name of the Lord shall be saved" (Acts 2:21). I am calling on You. I pray and ask Jesus to come into my heart and be Lord over my life according to Romans 10:9-10. "If thou shalt confess with thy mouth the Lord Jesus, and shalt believe in thine heart that God hath raised him from the dead, thou shalt be saved. For with the heart man believeth unto righteousness; and with the mouth confession is made unto salvation." I do that now. I confess that Jesus is Lord, and I believe in my heart that God raised Him from the dead.

I am now reborn! I am a Christian — a child of Almighty God! I am saved! You also said in Your Word, "If ye then, being evil, know how to give good gifts unto your children: HOW MUCH MORE shall your heavenly Father give the Holy Spirit to them that ask him?" (Luke 11:13). I'm also asking You to fill me with the Holy Spirit. Holy Spirit, rise up within me as I praise God. I fully expect to speak with other tongues as You give me the utterance (Acts 2:4). In Jesus' Name. Amen!

Begin to praise God for filling you with the Holy Spirit. Speak those words and syllables you receive, not in your own language, but the language given to you by the Holy Spirit. You have to use your own voice. God will not force you to speak. Don't be concerned with how it sounds. It is a heavenly language!

Continue with the blessing God has given you and pray in the spirit every day.

You are a born-again, Spirit-filled believer. You'll never be the same!

Find a good church that boldly preaches God's Word and obeys it. Become a part of a church family who will love and care for you as you love and care for them.

We need to be connected to each other. It increases our strength in God. It's God's plan for us.

Make it a habit to watch the *Believer's Voice of Victory* television broadcast and become a doer of the Word, who is blessed in his doing (James 1:22-25).

About the Author

Canaan Land Ministries was founded in 1981 by Mac Gober. A violent and troubled Vietnam veteran, turned motorcycle hoodlum filled with guilt, anger and hate, Mac was radically changed by the love of Jesus Christ. He dedicated his life to helping thousands turn their lost and broken lives into productive and fruitful testimonies of God's mercy and compassion.

Mac and his wife, Sandra, took the first steps toward fulfilling their dream of Canaan Land Ministries by bringing hurting young people, as Mac had once been, into their small, rented home, sharing God's love and helping turn lives around. They believed God to fulfill their dream of opening a large facility that would enable them to minister to more hurting young men. God miraculously led them to the beautiful property in Autaugaville, Ala., today's home of Canaan Land Ministries.

Through the years, with the help of committed staff, partners and friends, Mac and Sandra invested countless hours of love and dedication to make Canaan Land Ministries a successful nonprofit, nondenominational, love-filled Christian home and year-long training program for men with life-controlling problems. Men learn spiritual, emotional and vocational skills to help ensure success in their callings, on the job and with their families. Since Mac's own life was profoundly changed by his encounter with Jesus Christ and the power of His Word, the program is God centered and Word-of-God infused to bring that same transforming power into the lives of hurting and wounded men battling substance abuse, alcoholism or other addictions.

Today, Mac and Sandra's legacy continues at Canaan Land Ministries. Their life-changing program is free of charge to students and their families, and is continuing to grow. A Canaan Land Ministries facility opened in Mapleton, Australia, in 2009, where thousands more hurting men will experience the joy and freedom of living in the Promised Land of new life in Jesus Christ!

We're Here for You!®

Your growth in God's WORD and victory in Jesus are at the very center of our hearts. In every way God has equipped us, we will help you deal with the issues facing you, so you can be the **victorious overcomer** He has planned for you to be.

The mission of Kenneth Copeland Ministries is about all of us growing and going together. Our prayer is that you will take full advantage of all The LORD has given us to share with you.

Wherever you are in the world, you can watch the *Believer's Voice of Victory* broadcast on television (check your local listings), the Internet at kcm.org or on our digital Roku channel.

Our website, **kcm.org,** gives you access to every resource we've developed for your victory. And, you can find contact information for our international offices in Africa, Asia, Australia, Canada, Europe, Ukraine and our headquarters in the United States.

Each office is staffed with devoted men and women, ready to serve and pray with you. You can contact the worldwide office nearest you for assistance, and you can call us for prayer at our U.S. number, +1-817-852-6000, 24 hours every day!

We encourage you to connect with us often and let us be part of your everyday walk of faith!

Jesus Is LORD!

Kenneth & Gloria Copeland

Kenneth and Gloria Copeland